A Century of Philosophy

A Century of Philosophy

Hans-Georg Gadamer
in Conversation with Riccardo Dottori

Translated by Rod Coltman
with Sigrid Koepke

continuum
NEW YORK • LONDON

2004

The Continuum International Publishing Group Inc
15 East 26th Street, New York, NY 10010

The Continuum International Publishing Group Ltd
The Tower Building, 11 York Road, London SE1 7NX

Originally published as *Die Lektion des Jahrhunderts:*
Ein philosophischer Dialog mit Riccardo Dottori
© 2000 by LIT Verlag, Münster, Hamburg, London

English translation © 2003 by
The Continuum International Publishing Group

Printed in the United States of America

Library of Congress Cataloging-in-Publication Data

Gadamer, Hans Georg, 1900-2002
    [Lektion des Jahrhunderts. English]
    A century of philosophy / Hans-Georg Gadamer in conversation with
  Riccardo Dottori ; translated by Rod Coltman with Sigrid Koepke.
      p. cm.
    Includes bibliographical references and index.
    ISBN 0-8264-1524-5 (hardcover : alk. paper)
    1. Gadamer, Hans Georg, 1900- –Interviews. 2. Philosophers –
  Germany–Interviews. 3. Philosophy, Modern–20th century.
  I. Dottori, Riccardo. II. Title.
  B3248.G34A5 2003
  193–dc22

                                 2003016554

Cover art:
Dora Mittenzwei
ὁ φιλόσοφος αὐτός
Acrylic on canvas, 2000 (190 x 290cm)
The painting hangs in the Klaus-Tschira-Stiftung, Heidelberg

Contents

Translator's Acknowledgments

I want to thank Sigrid Koepke for her efficient translations of both the introduction and the conclusion to this text and especially for her inestimable help in deciphering the subtle idiomatic nuances of the interviews themselves. I would also like to thank Jamey Findling for bailing me out of a jam by doing a basic translation of some ten pages of the text. In spite of the generous and extremely welcome aid of my colleagues, however, I take full responsibility for any errors that may have cropped up during the course of translating this book.

ROD COLTMAN

Introduction

These conversations with Hans-Georg Gadamer, which took place in 1999–2000, cannot be understood without a brief overview of the thirty years that I have known Hans-Georg Gadamer. I want to take the liberty, therefore, of beginning this book with an autobiographical prologue that will serve as a lead-in to the theme of the interviews. At the end of these philosophical conversations, the reader will find an epilogue inspired by the portrait of Hans-Georg Gadamer by the artist Dora Mittenzwei, which appears on the cover of this book.

My first encounter with Hans-Georg Gadamer took place in the winter of 1969 when I relocated from Tübingen to Heidelberg. Back then, I had a research stipend and I was working in the field of modern philosophy, specifically on the philosophy of Hegel and on the revolutionary rupture in the philosophical thought of the nineteenth century as it is discussed in the works of Feuerbach, Kierkegaard, and Marx. While Gadamer, at that point, had become well known, he still was not as famous as Heidegger, Jaspers, Sartre, or the other writers who worked on questions of phenomenology, existentialism, and neo-Marxism. My decision to move to Heidelberg was influenced by the fact that the course listings for the following semester at the University of Heidelberg offered a seminar by Gadamer on the second book of Hegel's *Science of Logic,* the so-called "Logic of Essence." Not only does the authentic basis of the Hegelian system show itself in this work, but it was also precisely what I was working at the time. Moreover, Ernst Tugendhat, an assistant of Karl Tugendhat, the professor under whom I had studied previously, had also gone to Heidelberg just recently. Tugendhat, having been called to Heidelberg as a full professor, had announced that he would be giving a very interesting seminar on the concept of time that was to pay special attention to the writings of Augustine. I had met with Tugendhat shortly before my planned departure from Tübingen, when he was visiting old friends in that city. Being a very sociable and generous man who knew me quite well, Tugendhat informed me that neither he nor Gadamer (who at this point had already retired) would be conducting the seminars that had been announced in the course listings. "What should I do now?" I thought. "Should I reverse my decision and not go to Heidelberg?" "Calm down," said Tugendhat. "Even if Gadamer doesn't lecture on Hegel's *Logic* this year, he certainly will do so in the future. He's a dedicated pedagogue, and he won't stop conducting lectures and seminars so quickly." Indeed, in the following years this turned out to be prophetic; Gadamer gave his last lecture in 1985 — that is to say, seventeen years later. And when he ended his teaching duties — at the age of eighty-five — he did so in order to dedicate his time to the publication of his works, a task that he finished ten years later.

With Tugendhat's advice in mind, I decided to move to Heidelberg after all. I was drawn by the expectation of working with Tugendhat again and was hoping that, eventually, he would offer a lecture or seminar on the concept of time in Augustine. However, in Tugendhat's case, things changed. He completely abandoned his plans and, instead, dove headlong into the study of analytical philosophy in order to confront and compare the metaphysical problematic that he had encountered in Aristotle with analytical philosophy and develop it further. This huge undertaking eventually culminated in the publication of the lectures that he gave in Heidelberg under the title "Introduction to Analytical Philosophy." As far as Gadamer was concerned, things developed differently and, I must say, in a most advantageous manner for me. Instead of the seminar on Hegelian logic, Gadamer read Kant's "Third Critique," *The Critique of Judgment,* which constitutes the starting point for Gadamer's hermeneutical philosophy and, specifically, his foundational work, *Truth and Method.*

At the time, I was not thoroughly familiar with *Truth and Method.* While the work was already perceived as an interesting and important book, I had merely scanned it without making an effort to work through it meticulously. Compared to many others, however, this book was an easy read because it was written in a fluid, concise, and elegant style — the very style that, even apart from its content, eventually made *Truth and Method* a classic of the twentieth century. Gadamer's seminar allowed me to engage deeply in a reading of the text and, at the same time, presented an entirely different way of thinking. Truly new ways of thinking opened up for me in this seminar — not only in view of a new conception of the aesthetic but of metaphysical and existential experience as well. Few other lectures I had attended during my studies and research work had such a fundamental impact on me. I can recall only two other seminars that might measure up: One was the very first lecture I attended at the University of Rome where Guido Calogero had invited Raymond Klibansky, the famous expert on neo-Platonism and, in particular, the "Plato latinus" (the medieval translation of the *Theologia platonica*) and the commentaries on Proclus and Parmenides. The discussions between Calogero and Klibansky left me with impressions similar to those I came away with from the seminar in Heidelberg. Then, four years later, I attended Derrida's lectures on Kant's *Critique of Judgment* in Paris at the *Ecole des Hautes Etudes*. While these were also very interesting, they nevertheless did not reach the same level as the seminar in Heidelberg. We must consider, of course, that this was Gadamer's own fundamental theme, and (as we are dealing with Kant here) we should also remember that Gadamer and his entire school of thought stood squarely within the tradition of German philosophy, which was not the case with Derrida.

Indeed, I was surprised by the remarkably high level of the discussions in Gadamer's seminar. I should mention that all of the participants in the seminar would, in later years, hold the most important chairs of philosophy in Germany. But I was most impressed by the figure of Gadamer himself, by his friendliness and his attentiveness in the discussions, by the seriousness with which he entertained every opinion that was expressed, by his ability to follow other people's ideas as if he were always ready to learn something from them, and his constant willingness to question himself and his own opinions — even when the discussion had already made considerable headway. Whenever Gadamer was convinced of his position, however, then it was very difficult to dissuade him from his line of reasoning. I must say that my small contributions to the discussions in this and subsequent seminars were often adopted. And this is how the commonality of thinking developed between us, a commonality that bound me to him for decades to come.

Of course, the important thing is not to be convinced of one's own ideas and defend them to the death, but, instead, one has to keep on questioning them without insisting on having the last word. "It is a poor hermeneut who needs to have the last word," Gadamer resolutely asserts in his demanding autobiography. Gadamer held himself to this self-interpretation by always giving the other a chance to have his say. This is why whenever one visited Gadamer the discussions would last the entire afternoon and on into the evening, or deep into the night if they began in the evening. I remember one story that was related to me by my Chilean friend, Alfonso Gómez-Lobo, an expert on Plato who is now teaching at Georgetown University in Washington. When Gomez-Lobo visited Gadamer's house for the first time, he engaged Gadamer in a discussion that lasted until the late evening. As my friend was leaving, he tried to apologize for the long conversation, and Gadamer replied, "Nonsense. You know perfectly well that one Platonist can never inconvenience another Platonist." Indeed, for a Platonist there is no other path to the knowledge of truth than the dialogue.

Truth is a concept that had become deeply compromised in the twentieth century, especially when we consider its history. And it is this history that will occupy us in the interview below as a testament to the second half of that century — a half-century that saw fundamental changes in European culture and is worthy of our ruminations.

If my arrival in Heidelberg — that city on the Neckar with its castle and its old bridge, the city that shaped the heart of German Romanticism — evoked in me the semblance of a deep immersion into the past of German culture, then the present exerted no less powerful an attraction on me. These were the years of the student protests, and I found myself smack in the middle of them there. As a holder of a research stipend, I had one foot in the camp of the students and the other in that of those who were teaching them. Many of these were on the side of the students — among them, in Heidelberg, the above-mentioned Tugendhat. Thirty years later, despite the most disparate possible appraisals, we cannot escape the impression of a collective insanity that affected both sides — an insanity that always occurs among those who are fighting for their myths, as was the case here. Every opportunity was ripe for organizing a protest, a demonstration, or an uprising and for provoking a corresponding counter-reaction from the other side. In Heidelberg once, it so happened that, after a student demonstration in front of the America-house and an organized protest there, the police themselves made an "attack" on the university. They beat up any student who happened to be there — even those unsuspecting students who just wanted to go home peacefully from the events after a class.

In reality, despite the ideological motive of putting on a show of class struggle and the revolution of the proletariat, this protest was the product of an affluent and consumer-driven society. It was no accident that the principal activists were students who came mainly from the bourgeoisie and not the working classes. In point of fact, one should not confuse this protest at the end of the 1960s in Europe with the labor union struggle that flared up across the whole decade and that, on the wave of the development of the postwar economy and the subsequent demand for work, had fundamentally altered the situation of the working classes. What the student protest changed was primarily habits and customs within the society and the family, so-called general morality, attitudes, that is, toward sexuality and every form of authority. More than anything else, it was a protest of the youth against any kind of authority — a protest that entailed a radical change in our habitual way life. But, as a consequence, it also brought with it the depressing spread of drugs, illegal abortions, and a great psychic instability that stimulated an enormous surge in psychoanalysis.

In February of 1969, in this combustible political climate, it happened that Heidegger came to visit Gadamer on the occasion of his birthday. Consequently, all the seminar participants received a written invitation to take part in an evening seminar with Heidegger at Gadamer's home. The seminar (on the topic "Art and Space") began at eight o'clock in the evening. The topic was a reference to the lecture of the same name that Heidegger had held in a gallery in Neuchâtel on the occasion of an exhibition by the sculptor Chillida. Prior to this seminar, however, Heidegger had been invited to hold a public lecture, which was held in the afternoon in a lecture hall of the university. The hall (the Heuscheuer) was overflowing with students, while the professors from the faculty sat in the front row, Gadamer and Löwith among them. The latter had already become emeritus some years ago and was now the dominant figure of the philosophy department. He also delivered the birthday address to Gadamer and made a few introductory remarks about Heidegger's lecture. Unfortunately, the speech turned out not to be very exciting for the students. Even though, being a Jew, Löwith had to go into the exile during the Third Reich, he represented a rather conservative attitude. He spoke about how the essence of the university found itself, as did the culture at large, in decline because of mass production and industry. I was impressed by the fact that, while the other professors applauded everything he said, Tugendhat, dismayed by the speech, noticeably abstained from applause, even though he was standing very close to Löwith.

After a brief word of thanks by Gadamer in which he underscored the limitations of education ("the calcification of the human being") but also his dedication to it ("should one not be what one has become?"), he finally allowed Heidegger to speak. His voice was low and a little hoarse or perhaps intentionally hoarse so as to lend expression, so to speak, to the strain of old age and the fact of having to speak at such an occasion. The fascination that his words radiated was still quite strong, even if it differed fundamentally from that speculative vehemence of his famous Marburg lectures, which Gadamer so often described. This was not because he could not follow current events, nor was it the onset of absent-mindedness. Rather, his entire speech was a defense of contemporary philosophy, especially phenomenology. There is always phenomenology in every true philosophy, he claimed, whenever it wants to make genuine contact with and have a serious confrontation with things. He then ended his talk with the following words: "In our contemporary history, the words of Marx have never been more relevant; he tells us that the task of philosophy can no longer be to explain the world but to change it. If we wish to change the world, however, we must know to what end we would change it, and that, in turn, only philosophy can tell us." At this point everyone applauded — students and professors alike. Also among them was Leoluca Orlando, who is now mayor of Palermo and is known for his campaign against the Mafia. He studied and did research in Heidelberg just as I did. Together, we applauded enthusiastically, and he even recalls this event in his book about Palermo and describes it as particularly formative for his life.

With all the attention paid to Marx, it was only natural that one should develop just as strong an interest in Hegel as his antithesis. It was not just that Marx was his student, but Lenin had also drawn his basic reflections in equal parts from Marx's *Capital* and Hegel's *Logic*. What Hegel proposed was essentially a contemplation of history from the viewpoint of reason and the self-knowledge of the human being, a justification of reason in history, or, in any case, a justification of reason in all its shadings and its dialectic — the dialectic of power and servitude, of enlightenment and superstitions, of rebellion and consensus. It really had less to do with a justification of reason in history — or, more precisely, God in history — than it did a pure justification of history itself, understood as a progressive realization of human freedom. This was the meaning of his concluding reflection on reality, the ontological reflection. Was all of this just a legitimation of the status quo, of the Prussian state and its constitutional monarchy? Or, even worse, was it (as Marx thought) a legitimation of the oppression of the working classes in the early days of industrial society? This was the debate that Kierkegaard and Marx took up again in their basic critiques of Hegelian philosophy and its will to systematization. This was also the motive around which my work revolved, and it was decisive for my interest in Hegel. It also stirred the general interest of the students and intellectuals of the time. All of this reached its high point in the following year, in the Winter semester of which Gadamer finally lectured on the second book of the Hegel's *Logic,* and which was to end for me in surprising way.

Toward the end of the seminar, we were discussing the fundamental concept of Hegelian metaphysics, the concept of ontological reflection, which had its origins in Hegel's youthful writings and culminated in Kant's concept of reflective and determinative judgment, which we had discussed earlier in the seminar. I presented a *Referat* on this topic toward the end of the semester. During the last session, we expected a retrospective review of the entire seminar from Gadamer. But it was precisely in this last session — which fell, of all days, on the eleventh of February, Gadamer's birthday — that Heidegger entered the room with him and took a seat beside him. Gadamer took the floor, and after he had summarized the conclusions of the entire seminar and the *Referat* that I had presented, he closed with a quotation from Heidegger's book on Nietzsche. In the quoted passage, Heidegger rightly portrayed the Hegelian concept of ontological reflection as the quintessence of modern philosophy. But this metaphysics of subjectivity, which leads into a metaphysics of history from the perspective of the self-realization of human freedom, subsequently finds its end in Nietzsche's own metaphysics of the absolute will to power. In all of this, however, one unambiguously recognizes the total appropriation of the real on the part of technology and, with it, the most absolute nihilism, the absence and devaluation of all values.

The question was then passed on to Heidegger, who took it upon himself to defend this quotation and its theses and to come to a conclusion. I took note of all of this and later published it.[1] The most

1. See Hans-Georg Gadamer, *La dialettica di Hegel, con due lettere di M. Heidegger ad H.-G. Gadamer,* trans. and commentary by Riccardo Dottori (Turin: Marietti, 1973; 2d corrected and rev. ed., Genua: Marietti 1996), 189–202. German edition: "Über das Verhältnis Hegel, Heidegger, Gadamer: Die Begegnung in Heidelberg" in *Bijdragen* 6 (1977).

interesting thesis that Heidegger put forward on this occasion was that he never understood why, for the Greeks, being [or essence, *das Wesen*], the *on*, developed into the *hen*, the one, in exactly the same way that, in Kant, being [*das Sein*] developed into the one *on* the basis of the synthetic unity of apperception. Ultimately, this is what the whole of philosophical reflection (understood as a transcendental reflection) aims at, and, according to Heidegger, this is the reason that even the logical application of reason is tied to the concept of unity. This is why transcendental reflection becomes the basis of Hegel's ontology — all of what is real is consequently grounded in this ultimate unity of reason, and this is not only why the real appears to us, it is even why history itself is legitimized. This is also the basis of the fundamental concept in Marx's *Capital,* the concept of *value* (which ensues from *being* [*das Wesen*]). And all of this culminates in Nietzsche's concept of the will to power.

I went away from this session agitated, and it took a long time for the meaning of this encounter with Heidegger to become clear to me — only later did I also understand Gadamer's original intention. It was not just a matter of rehabilitating Heidegger's stature or an attempt to retrieve him from the isolation into which he had been advised to go after his dismissal from the University of Freiburg. It was rather about the revival of his thinking, about going back to the path he had walked in his long dialogue with the ideas of the Greeks and the moderns. This path led directly into that tremendous provocation that expressed itself in Nietzsche's thinking. He came upon it precisely in the years of National Socialism, and this plunged him into that deep crisis from which he sought to escape through the ideas of Hölderlin.

Nevertheless, on the basis of all of this, one question arises spontaneously: Does this discourse actually succeed in comprehending the meaning of history, or is it merely about a new philosophical structure? Does all of this find a parallel in the actual history of society, and is there any real meaning in the history of the philosophers (either the good ones or the bad ones)? Maybe the prominence they attained is a consequence of how much they actually knew about what happens before their very eyes, that is, how much they knew about real historical processes. Maybe that is what Heidegger meant by saying that phenomenology forms the kernel of every authentic philosophy. Perhaps he himself comprehended how much he was responsible for (vis-à-vis real historical processes) in his original restriction of phenomenology to the structural analyses of existence or the existence of the human being in the world. Maybe the fact that he had not considered this in advance was also a reason for his succumbing to a completely mistaken understanding of National Socialism. This is possibly how that reorientation in his thinking began, the one that brought him back again to a different kind of phenomenology that no longer posed the question of being (in Husserl's wake) from the viewpoint of internal time consciousness but from the much more broadly construed perspective of the history of being, which is tantamount to the history of Western culture. He tried, as Hegel had done before him, to completely disclose the actual developmental stages of history. These considerations brought Hegel to his main thesis of recognizing reason within history and thereby demonstrating the justification or legitimation of God in history — whereas contemplating history led Nietzsche and Heidegger to their visions of a decadent nihilism. All of this is irrelevant, of course, if one takes into account the fact that after the experiences of the twentieth century we can no longer pursue philosophy without worrying about what actually happens to us instead of simply posing the question of being as such, as metaphysics has always done. This is perhaps what Gadamer, in contrast to Heidegger, has always understood. To know how to pull on the threads of everything that surrounds us so as to discover the web from which reality is made, this spider's web in which we are caught — this was Max Scheler's advice (on a visit to Marburg) to the young student, Gadamer, who was very impressed by it.

Nevertheless, the respective roles that Heidegger and Jaspers have played in the history of our century — each in his own way and with differing results — are not without significance. After a period of friendship and cooperation, the two found themselves in opposing situations once again as the storm of National Socialism lifted. Heidegger now saw a chance for a renaissance of pure German culture, and he remained rooted in this idea, even without being able to imagine what was to come. Jaspers had a Jewish wife and therefore did not share Heidegger's views, even as they kept working together on the idea of university reform. And it was this same idea that Heidegger advocated as rector in his 1933 inaugural speech. But Jaspers' cultured and refined intellect warned him against what was brewing. Heidegger was also very cultured, but he was essentially a farmer and a mystic of a mysticism without God, whom he had lost and for whom he found himself constantly searching.

He noticed for the first time that he had succumbed to an error when he was called to Berlin. Jaspers, who had already been hoping for such an appointment, encouraged him to it accept it. So he went to Berlin in the hope of meeting Hitler and building a relationship with him similar to the one that existed between Giovanni Gentile and Mussolini. He did not even succeed in meeting the appropriate minister, however, and so he came back to his birthplace in Meßkirch to ponder this disappointment. Thus he wrote to his half-Jewish friend, Elisabeth Blochmann, "The whole thing would have been abysmal anyway." The fact that he then still took up the rectorate and subsequently set in motion that discourse that Croce characterized as "stupid and, above all, servile," should indicate, however, that his delusion persisted, at least in a small way. This was certainly not a good example of intelligence or political vision, but one should not attribute it to a deplorable careerism or anti-Semitic conviction. His love of Hannah Arendt and his friendship with Elisabeth Blochmann and his Jewish assistants and colleagues who stayed on during the war demonstrate this eloquently — as does his resignation from the rectorate after only a nine-month term in office. Neither can one say that either his life or his philosophy served or influenced the history of National Socialism in any way.

Jaspers stayed in Germany, although he was released from his teaching duties and sent into retirement. He did not want to be separated from his wife; he preferred to weather the dangers with her, and this is why he seems an entirely different figure to us compared to Heidegger and more discerning as well. But he also found himself in a different situation, even if it was by no means a more enviable one. Nevertheless, his behavior toward Heidegger was not exactly praiseworthy during the period of the French occupation when he wrote to the de-Nazification commission at the University of Freiburg saying that, even though Heidegger may be the greatest philosophical mind in Germany, a few years' hiatus from teaching would do him some good. And the illusions that he created for himself during the initial phase of the Federal Republic of Germany were not so discerning either. To hear Gadamer tell it, his judgment of Heidegger and his decision to begin a self-imposed exile in Switzerland were politically naive and even moralistic. Nevertheless, the two were finally reconciled, and Hegel's expression, "The wounds of the spirit heal without leaving scars," was borne out. The roles of the preeminent philosophical protagonists to romp about on the German stage of the twentieth century should not be considered on the basis of their individual histories or their political roles but exclusively on the basis of their roles as thinkers. Like so many others, both of them were victims of National Socialism.

The role of the philosophical protagonist has been expanded upon by Gadamer in the second half of the century. Gadamer only brought out his fundamental work, *Truth and Method,* at the age of sixty. Not only was he already well known by this time (through his writings on Platonic philosophy and his other philosophical essays on modern poetry), but he had also matured, especially through his teaching duties as a *Privatdozent* in Marburg and, above all, in Leipzig. He arrived there in 1935 and taught there until after the war. He became rector at the beginning of the Russian occupation, and he even stayed on during the first years of the German Democratic Republic. His inaugural speech as rector, an office that he occupied with conviction and passion, did not please Jaspers ("now he is a Communist," Jaspers is supposed to have commented), and it occasioned the cold shoulder with which Gadamer was received in Heidelberg and Jaspers' break with him, which he describes in the interview. But in 1995, when Gadamer was made an honorary citizen of the city of Leipzig, a former student wrote about the enthusiasm with which Gadamer's speech had been received in 1945. The speech had been delivered in front of the university to representatives of the political authority, the city administrators, and a large number of citizens while Russian soldiers on horseback surrounded the square. The student told me, "Only Gadamer could give such a speech. We had the feeling that he was defending us."

In this speech, Gadamer claimed (as he never did again) that, since the power of the cultural tradition had proven too weak to save the country from the barbarism and murderous insanity of National Socialism, one should no longer look to the old, but rather to the new. Then, however, he referred to what had always been and would remain the key point of his hermeneutic practice — the factuality of work, the uncertainty that feeds off of itself, the prudence of the scholar (*phronesis*) that results in unconditional confidence in what one has discovered, and, lastly, the simplicity of one's conduct, which leads to tolerance and true solidarity. We can summarize these in a single concept — wisdom.

In the era of post-historicism, the seriousness with which one conducts scholarly work and confronts a text has to be fundamentally guided by and understood through a personal engagement with it. There are no rules for interpretation other than the seriousness of an interpretation that continuously questions itself to the point of conviction that one has reached something essential. However, one should never think that one has reached any kind of objective interpretation in which the text, the subject, and the historical period resolve themselves completely. The only guarantee against the dangers of historical relativism is being aware of the ineluctable historicity of all our interpretations. And, according to Gadamer, this is basically what he learned from Heidegger: If we are directly conscious of the historicity of our being, then we are just as far beyond any real historical ontology as we are any relativism. This certainly holds true for all interpretations of the world and, therefore, for the decisive liquidation of all previous ontology and metaphysics, without thereby losing the fundamental claim or the truth of the determining historical horizon, which legitimates itself by means of a fusion of horizons. Reading a text becomes the model for reading the world, and philosophical hermeneutics becomes philosophy or hermeneutic philosophy.

Gadamer's realistic, skeptical, and tolerant demeanor, and his natural gift for diplomacy allowed him to survive three revolutions unharmed — namely, those of the Weimar Republic, the Third Reich, and communism — " . . . three revolutions that changed nothing," Gadamer tells us in his autobiography. Psychologically speaking, he remained undamaged due to his self-confidence; physically speaking, he was saved by polio, the disease he acquired as an adult before the war began. The small concessions that he was forced to make never touched the core of his personality. He never succumbed to flattery or careerism, and he never had to pay the high price of self-denial for the career that he nevertheless forged for himself in those years. As Hegel warned, "a mended sock is better than no sock at all — but, this is not true in the case of self-confidence." This is how Gadamer honorably maintained all of his contacts with Jaspers, his Jewish friends in Marburg, with Jakob Klein, Leo Strauss, and Karl Löwith. After everything had blown over, he even tried to get Löwith to come to Heidelberg with him. And, in the same vein, as soon as the horrors of National Socialism had passed he immediately tried to contact his first teacher, Heidegger, again.

In spite of his apparent conservativism (of which Habermas had accused him from early on) and in spite of his confrontation with

Habermas on the subject of "Hermeneutics and the Critique of Ideology," thanks to his disposition, Gadamer never erred in those fundamental questions such as the relationship between authority and critique (which had been the starting point of the debate), or the concept of social consensus (which depends entirely on the acknowledgment of authority), or the relationship between tradition and emancipation. With the winding down of the ideological struggles and the concomitant demise of the Eastern European regimes, Gadamer was proven right with respect to a question that is fundamental for hermeneutic philosophy — the truth that remains is the truth of our cultural and civil tradition and not that which manifests itself in the results of the scientific method. Any authority that truly is an authority and is acknowledged as such is based upon this truth; and only if the authority is acknowledged will it be an authentic one. Otherwise, as Gadamer maintains as early as 1972, and as the experience of history has shown, that authority will deteriorate; and the recent demise of the Eastern European states has proven Gadamer right once again. Despite all the criticisms that one might levy against it, the authority of our tradition, as the basis of all established or political authority, is essentially the supporting ground of social consensus. Its strength does not lie so much in standing up to those criticisms as in making any critique possible; for every critique and every discussion presupposes the supporting consensus that makes possible every civil discussion, every dialogue, be it among various social or political groups or among various belief systems, religions, or ideologies.

This was the lesson that Gadamer taught to us all, including the students in 1968 and especially Habermas; for their confrontation hinged mainly upon their respective conceptions of authority and tradition. Habermas, by the way, was the first to understand this lesson, even in relation to the upheaval that the student movements had created in Frankfurt. He eventually left the university and the heated atmosphere of Frankfurt in the turbulent years between 1972 and 1975 in order to withdraw to an institution that he co-founded with Tugendhat called the "Institute for the Study of Living Conditions in the Technical Scientific World" at Lake Starnberg near Munich. In reality, his stay there did not last very long, and Tugendhat went to Berlin at the same time that Habermas was returning to Frankfurt. By that time, things had changed again at the universities — peace had returned, and all those bewildered souls once again needed a certain security. Richard Rorty, who had just published *Philosophy and the Mirror of Nature,* was invited to teach in Heidelberg. Neo-pragmatism, which Richard Bernstein even saw latent in Gadamer, had come from the American scene and had begun to find adherents in Germany.

Gadamer's student Michael Theunissen, who had openly sympathized with the leftist scene, moved from Heidelberg to Berlin. But the intellectual atmosphere had changed even in Berlin. After various attempts at a new metaphysics had run aground, the critique of metaphysics disappeared not so much from enlightened philosophical consciousness as from the pages of existentialism and analytic philosophy. Everyone in America and in Europe was now preoccupied with ethics. In Tübingen, Tugendhat already had been interested in the existential problematic, and, to keep up with the times, he returned partially to his original topic in his new book, *Selbstbesinnung und Selbstbestimmung,* in which he still retained an echo of Kierkegaard's anti-Hegelian polemic.

When the fires of the ideological struggles that had drenched the century in blood and had found their final echo in the student protests had been extinguished, and when everyone had now become preoccupied with ethics, people were also discovering Gadamer's first book, *Plato's Dialectical Ethics.* The book was Gadamer's habilitation thesis under Heidegger and had essentially been conceived either as an introduction to Aristotle's ethics or as a disclosure of the commonalities between Aristotle and Plato. Eventually, it initiated the so-called "rehabilitation of practical philosophy," which began in Germany in the 1980s. This was a rediscovery of practical knowing as a special type of knowing that differed from the theoretical; it is a knowing that exists for its own sake and is, essentially, the only knowledge that can assist us in understanding and in making decisions regarding our private as well as our public or social lives. The concept of *phronesis,* wisdom, played a fundamental role here and found its genuine and real verification in the disastrous consequences of the ideological struggles.

It was Habermas himself who undertook the task of bringing this verification to its conclusion. The conception of truth that he attempted to reclaim was, in any case, not that of our cultural tradition, but rather that of a universal pragmatism, which he gradually developed toward a concept of communicative action. This concept also influenced the theory of the community of communication or communicative ethics developed by Habermas's colleague in Frankfurt,

Karl-Otto Apel. Gadamer has pointed out to us that every ethical principle of understanding can be traced back to the dialectical principle of Platonic philosophy. Ultimately, every ethics of discourse is grounded more on the desire for unity than on a supposed *a priori* of the community of communication. If, however, this orientation toward an ethics of discourse follows Gadamer's thinking, even to a small extent, then a total rapprochement with Gadamer — in part with the idea of a consensus grounded on authority, and in part with the sustaining value of tradition — can no longer be far off. It was his confrontation with American philosophy, with John Rawls's theory of justice, and with the turbulent discussions about the fundamental legal situation and the basic concepts of German and American democracy, that led Habermas to rediscover the value of tradition and historical context in relation to a purely rational mode of argumentation. In the debate about the legitimation of justice and, especially, the legitimation of norms, he realized that this was not established on the basis of *rational* argumentation alone, but also on the basis of the historical existence of the society and its norms as well as on the creative act of interpretation.

However, a renewed critique of Gadamer came from Habermas on the basis of an article written on the occasion of Gadamer's one-hundredth birthday. Gadamer supposedly loses the authentic claim to truth for philosophical assertions when they cannot be contradicted by facts, and he supposedly ignores the "instructive renunciation of the world."[2] According to Habermas, he simply holds fast to the heritage of our cultural tradition, which finds its model in the ideal of classical works of art or in works of literature and poetry, which are always self-referential and can never stand in contradiction to reality. In the aftermath of historicism, we have nothing left but the new "mysticism" of poetry. Moreover, because Gadamer relies, above all, on the persuasive power of words and therefore on rhetorical modes of argumentation, he positions himself between neo-pragmatism and deconstruction.

Needless to say, Gadamer offered no objection to this first accusation. Always citing the famous passage from Aristotle's *Poetics,* he never tired of repeating that history can only tell us how events occur, while poetry is more philosophical than history because it tells us how events could or should occurred. This is also the basis upon which he

2. [der "*belehrenden Widerruf der Welt*"]

grounds his defense of Hegel — reason cannot stand in contradiction to individual historical events. And however things might have happened or might still happen, the ultimate truth, which we can accept as the sole truth, is that which philosophy offers us, the truth that presents the progressive realization of human freedom through history. This, however, does not mean that how events occur is of little interest to us; on the contrary, it is highly important to us, because we have nothing else on which we can base the truth of our actions than on a renunciation of the facts.

Finally, the second objection is the one for which I will attempt to provide answers in our interview. Is a new mysticism possible in the aftermath of historicism? Is it this toward which our will to understand and our will to persuade are directed — if, that is, one ultimately understands the two as one and the same will toward a consensus? Is it perhaps this concrete consensus that humanity needs and that we need to acknowledge at the end of the twentieth century of the Christian era — a century that, on the one hand, has been marked by new experiences of art and scientific progress and that, on the other hand, has been marked even more by a terrible will to destruction and death? The last god, the god whose absence Heidegger so painfully perceived upon losing him — is this the hope that such a consensus could still be possible? Is this last god the last hope that remains, the final inheritance of a bygone metaphysics and the thing that will survive its destruction?

A consensus among all the forms of faith and all the great religions about what they all have in common seems to be, for Gadamer, the last possibility for saving humanity after a century that lived on myths and, in its struggles for these myths and these ideologies, stained itself with blood. This consensus is certainly not the fruit of philosophical deliberations — even if these deliberations point to such a possibility. But neither is it a question of the consensus that results from persuasion and from individual dialogue. It is indeed a question of a dialogue, but one between the great religions, one that throws into relief what they all have in common — that sense for the divine that is the basis of them all — and which springs from the knowledge of our own finitude, our awe in the face of the origin of life and our disquieting perception of the extreme limit of death. These two basic instincts of our soul are also the basis for any metaphysics, any question of being and non-being, our feeling of awe in the face of life or, in the case of Aristotle, our astonishment. In Heidegger's case, this would be our angst in the face of non-being or in the face of death — an angst that goes even deeper because, as Gadamer says, after Europe had opened the way to peaceful coexistence following the tragic experiences of the past century the whole of humanity seems to have found itself threatened.

The twentieth century has just ended. Gadamer, who lived through the whole of it, with all its horrors and all its mistakes, apparently puts no hope in anything new other than the last god. His hermeneutical philosophy, as a philosophy that reflects human finitude, with an eye fixed upon all that we have constructed and that we still bring to our cultural tradition, maintains a view that is confident and open to what is. His life blessed him with one hundred years of experience, unique for a philosopher, especially if we consider which century it was. His cup is well filled, not only with lived experiences, but also with ripened wisdom. If we really want to find a key term in his philosophy, then we should not simply say "hermeneutics" or "interpretation," but rather, as he himself said over and over again, *phronesis,* "wisdom." With this interview, we are trying to benefit from his wisdom in the hope that it will infect us all and also in the hope that one of Hegel's dictum's will prove to be true — that the wounds of the spirit heal without leaving scars.[3]

It pleases me that the artist, Dora Mittenzwei (Heidelberg), has given us permission to use her Gadamer portrait, which was unveiled in March of 2001. I will follow this personal homage with some of my thoughts. I want to express my sincere thanks to Hans-Georg Gadamer for his openness, the artist for her willingness, numerous helpers in Heidelberg, Rome, and, last but not least, the LIT publishing house.

RICCARDO DOTTORI
Rome

3. Translated from the Italian into German by Tobias Güthner, Britta Hentschel, and Daniela Wolf. [Translated from the German into English by Sigrid Koepke and Rod Coltman.]

1
Phronesis:
A Philosophy of Finitude

D.: The twentieth century seems to have closed with a negative balance with respect to the question of being, and it seems to have pulled all the questions that Western thinking deemed worthy of asking along with it — particularly the questions of the meaning of life and the mystery of death. The first question that we would like to pose, therefore, is: What remains valid within the philosophical and cultural tradition, or what is still to be salvaged from its highest invention — metaphysics — after the two attempts at dismantling it emanating from Heidegger and analytical philosophy?

G.: Perhaps we can attempt an answer by starting from the ideas that Heidegger and I developed. At the outset, the young Heidegger received his metaphysics from a Scholastic or Catholic position and developed it further from there. When I first encountered Heidegger, this development was already in full swing. When he later went to Marburg, it was falling back a little more in line with the expectations of a Protestant — I should say, in line with the figure of a Luther or a Melanchthon. From the perspective of Protestantism, a metaphysics is clearly unnecessary. I remember quite well that what captivated me about Heidegger was not the resuscitation but the rethinking of metaphysics, and indeed in such a way that the question of existence became his theme and the questions of time and finitude along with it. Thus we have a philosophy of finitude, if you will, and a philosophy of temporality at the same time. What I had previously learned from Heidegger was his critique of Neo-Kantianism, and the figure standing behind this was Max Scheler. There was a congress with Scheler in Marburg in 1913, and the lecture he gave was a critique of Neo-Kantian idealism. This had the effect on Nicolai Hartmann (and consequently upon the Marburg school) of a kind of unintentional approximation to an ontological realism. This didn't convince me at all, for the critique of idealism then led into a metaphysical — even Thomistic — ontology of values.

Things were different in Heidegger's case, where, at the center of his book (along with his general impact and the thrust of his thinking) stood the questions of death, being toward death, and so on. Heidegger's book was no great event for us in Marburg. During five years of his lectures, we had already had a chance to follow the evolution of the book, which depended upon the analyses of temporality. I was trying to do something different at the time, something that Heidegger couldn't do at all, and this came out of my book, *Plato's Dialectical Ethics,* which served as my habilitation thesis. I was trying to come to philosophy along different paths, specifically, along the path of practical knowledge. What I later developed in the form of *phronesis* was already taking shape here. These essays (like, for example, the essay on practical knowing) show both what I was later to develop into that concept and what I didn't do at the time. But the decisive step was already taken in that, from that point on, even if I had wanted to follow Heidegger, I could no longer have accommodated him. I very clearly remember a draft of Heidegger's that hadn't been published and that I received from Natorp. It went missing, and one day it turned up again. I was very deeply impressed that this early piece was subsequently published in *Dilthey Studien* under the title "Phenomenological Interpretations of Aristotle: Indications of the Hermeneutic Situation." But, having read it again, I see that I could actually have established quite clearly that Heidegger wasn't really interested in practical knowledge or *phronesis* at all.

D.: But rather . . . ?

G.: But rather, being.

D.: So, you think that the question of being was removed from its usual Scholastic/ontological context, that is, from the question of the science of being as such, and from its respective regional ontologies, like psychology, cosmology, theology, so as to be put on a completely new basis, namely, on the basis of his own conception of human *Dasein,* which, along with Jaspers, he calls *existence,* the basic structure of which makes a disinterested and objectified view of being in the sense of the old metaphysics impossible for us. But, in his analysis of *Dasein,* didn't Heidegger proceed from his reading of Aristotle? Wasn't he essentially preoccupied with the *Nicomachean Ethics?*

G.: No, not all that much; no. If you look at it closely, he isn't really all that preoccupied with Aristotle. Obviously, he had been at one time. I even became initially aware of *phronesis,* the reasonableness of practical knowing, through Heidegger. But I subsequently found a better basis for *phronesis,* which I developed, not in terms of a virtue, but rather in terms of the dialogue.

D.: You were certainly very insistent on the concept of *phronesis,* which later became a key concept of your own philosophy, and you were especially insistent on that experience that you call hermeneutic experience. This central concept of the text of the *Nicomachean Ethics* was originally translated into Latin by the word *prudentia,* and you pointed out that the term *jurisprudentia* draws its origin from the judge constantly being confronted with the problem of applying the general law to the individual case, which always deviates from the general law and poses the problem of correct application. This correct application of the law is supposed to be guided precisely by *prudentia,* which is supposed to determine the appropriateness of the law to the specific case in a just manner so that the subsequent judgment corresponds to the criterion of *equitas* (Aristotelean *epieikeia*), balance. This well-balanced judicial decision then becomes the basis of future judgments — this is how the Latin *jurisprudentia,* jurisprudence, would have originated. Proceeding from this conception of *phronesis* as an application of the general law to the specific case, then, you invested the concept with a much broader meaning. Specifically, you pointed out that this just application of the law presupposes not only a knowledge of the means by which virtue and justice are to be effected but also a knowledge of the end. Above all, however, in this correct application of the general law to the specific case, you saw the universal problem of *interpretation,* which in turn becomes the general problem of hermeneutic philosophy. Thus you arrived at a concept that is meant to dissolve the concept of reason without its essential content getting lost. After this, *reasonableness* would be the more appropriate translation of *phronesis.* This is how you elevated *phronesis* to the level of the dialogue. Do you mean to say that, if we were to turn from Aristotle back toward Plato, then the Platonic viewpoint would not essentially have changed, or do you believe that both philosophers stand on a common basis?

G.: Of course! The meaning of all my work — the meaning that runs throughout my subsequent studies as well — was to show that, in spite of all the criticism of Aristotle, a flat opposition between Plato and Aristotle is not at all correct. In those days I was already beginning to see that, no, there is a much more intimate connection here, a connection that I was later able to substantiate quite well — even with *phronesis,* which is really a Platonic concept. So, more and more I found that Heidegger's inability to acknowledge the other was a point of weakness in him, and even by then I had already been talking out about this. It thus seemed clear to me how, through his analysis of existence, through his search for God, he hoped to come to a better philosophical justification of human existence in the sense of a Christian experience. Today, this initial insight of mine seems to be simply a fact; but it is also clear that this kind analysis and this conception of human existence leave the problem of the other unthought.

D.: But didn't Heidegger speak of *being-with* [*Mit-sein*], that is, being-there-with-the-other [*Mit-den-anderen-da-zu-sein*], and the *conscience* as excellent modes of human *Dasein* or structures of existence? Didn't these structures or these phenomena have something to do with a fundamental experience of the Thou?

G.: Yes, yes — we probably do read it rather one-sidedly; although, in the beginning, that business with the conscience alarmed me. Moreover, there is still the problem of the correspondence between *phronesis* and the Latin *prudentia* and the German word *Gewissen* [conscience]. Is *Gewissen* really the right translation? Bringing *phronesis* together with conscience or carrying the meaning of the first concept or phenomenon over into the second has never particularly convinced me. I was one of the first to follow Heidegger, and I was fascinated by his thinking; the course of my own thinking was actually established after my first encounter with Heidegger. Naturally, I was bowled over at first, and what the essay on the concept of being had to say was enormously liberating. I was twenty-two years old. In fact, this was carried so far that later commentators ascribed to me a certain primacy with respect to Heidegger, which, of course, was pure nonsense. It was, however, a very quick reception on my part. On the other hand, I have to say that Hartmann's, so to speak, objectivizing treatment of being was an absolutely untenable position for me.

D.: So you think it would be wrong to bring conscience into a close relationship with *phronesis?*

G.: Well, for Heidegger, the conscience is undoubtedly *not* the other, but is, rather, the puzzle of this "coming-to-find-oneself" [*Zu-sich-selbst-findens*].

D.: And *Mit-sein* . . . ?

G.: *Mit-sein* becomes really tenable only with an other. In any case, what I have gradually developed is not *Mit-sein* but *Miteinander* ["with-one-another"]. *Mit-sein,* for Heidegger, was a concession that he had to make, but one that he never really got behind. Indeed, even as he was developing the idea, his wasn't really talking about the other at all. *Mit-sein* is, as it were, an assertion about *Dasein,* which must naturally take *Mit-sein* for granted. I must say that conscience — having a conscience — no, that wasn't terribly convincing. "Care" [*die Sorge*] is always a concernfulness [*ein Besorgtsein*] about one's own being, and *Mit-sein* is, in truth, a very weak idea of the other, more a "letting the other be" than an authentic "being-interested-in-him."

D.: In your *Philosophical Apprenticeships* you report that had you already expressed this criticism to Heidegger in your Lisbon lecture (in 1943). You have also attempted to show that authentic *thrownness* [*Geworfenheit*], which, according to Heidegger, refers to the basic structure of human finitude, shows itself precisely in the phenomenon of the other.

G.: That was later, much later.

D.: Yes, you later lectured on it publicly; but that was a recollection of this original critique. When did you speak out about this to Heidegger for the first time?

G.: It was during my first encounter with Heidegger in Marburg, during the first discussions we had during the period in which he wrote *Being and Time.* The idea became completely clear to me at that time, and that's when I expressed my first criticisms.

D.: And what did Heidegger think of that? What was his reaction?

G.: Heidegger recognized (one had put it like this — he was far superior to me, after all), he recognized that I encompassed more with my idea of the other than he did with *Mit-sein. Mit-sein* is an atten-uation, because the "with" [*das Mit*] freely admits that the other is also *Dasein;* this "also," then, is, so to speak, its own justification for its conscience.

D.: It now seems clear to me. Was it from that point on that you brought your philosophy of finitude into play, and, was it from that point on that you ultimately established a perspective on the future of philosophy pro or contra metaphysics?

G.: Quite so! Although you ask the question as if I already had every-thing that would come later clearly before me. Nevertheless, that is essentially how it was. Nicolai Hartmann had referred me to the *Nicomachean Ethics.* He wanted me to write something. He presum-ably saw that he hadn't gotten enough from me and that the *Ethics* would lead me to the concept of value. And in that respect, of course, my task was a very difficult one. But it's even more true to say that it became a kind of catastrophe for me at this point. I tried to under-stand Aristotle in his different treatises on *hedone* and so forth, but I never really looked at this essay again. I do not even know whether it actually still exists. At the time, I only gave Hartmann a piece of it to show him what it looked like, and he was accustomed to being very satisfied with my, so to speak, strict conformity to his thinking. But, as I undertook this Aristotelean theme to satisfy the pressure from Hartmann, I realized that, even in my own mind, the project was completely misbegotten. I then tried to be ready with a perfect Heideggerian avoidance of the concept of value and failed. Unfortu-nately, the letters hadn't surfaced until recently, but Heidegger gave me a clear rebuke. So, with respect to these first sections, which had to do with *Being and Time,* or (better) with respect to the entire im-petus with which Heidegger freed me from Neo-Kantianism, I would say that, at first, it was really something that I wasn't prepared for. Heidegger said to me, "It doesn't amount to anything," so I gave it up. It really was a difficult crisis for me. Hartmann noticed that the traces of Heidegger's thinking that remained with me were not without consequences. He thus shared Heidegger's criticism of my effort (by that time I had given him something on *hedone*). "Well," Heidegger said to me, "it just doesn't amount to anything. You are simply not talented enough to do philosophical work. You need to learn Latin and Greek so you can teach." And I did that, too, for many years — as late as a year after Heidegger left Marburg.

D.: And then what happened? If I'm not mistaken, your effort consisted in giving up the concept of value and yet sticking firmly to Aristotle and to an ontological problematic or, at least, to an ethical one?

G.: Certainly. Only, you have to consider the fact that, at the time, I was going a completely new direction. I said, "No, I have to think about finishing soon." I had only three years to become a teacher, and that was very little time. I started out with Aristotle's *Protrepticus* and the whole debate about the development of Aristotelian philosophy in the three *Ethics*. The Jaeger thesis clarified absolutely nothing for me, and I must say, by the way, that my critique of Jaeger was entirely correct. Meanwhile, Jaeger's thesis has been completely abandoned. He is still read a little, but he is no longer discussed seriously. So, by that time, it was already untenable for me. It just wasn't correct. To start with, I saw a much more complicated relationship between pleasure and knowledge. Aristotle brought the topic of *agathon,* which unites the two, to bear on the concept of *phronesis,* which defined practical philosophy and yet was also a kind of revision of it at the same time. I think you're looking for something here that's very difficult for me to express. What did I do, then, when I came to Book Seven? I studied a lot of things about the *Protrepticus* and about Jaeger's position. I even received a stipend from the Deutschen Forschungsgemeinschaft through Jaeger's mediation. Later, of course, he rejected my criticism, but he recognized the thoroughness of my work. He treated me politely after that, especially since subsequent critics then came along who showed that the entire Aristotelian corpus doesn't accord with his chronological development. Now, these are the kinds of mistakes that we generally made in classical philology because we all thought that everything was written for the sake of writing books. This was incorrect; it was actually backwards — they wrote for the sake of teaching. Meanwhile, as you know, I personally came to think that the *Metaphysics* (for it was Jaeger's great accomplishment to show that the books of the *Metaphysics* are not really uniform) the *Metaphysics* is not a real book, not in its full scope, that is. This is quite clear. I am not so influential that I have become generally accepted in the Anglo-Saxon world. They still believe, after all, that one can accomplish more by contrasting Plato and Aristotle, while I am really searching more and more for the inner proximity between them. I now have to tell you what I did — I analyzed the *Protrepticus* in detail according to the Iamblichus text. I show just how the man worked. "What was he trying to do?" I asked. I then came to an absolutely clear conclusion — there was nothing in it at all about a critique of the doctrine of ideas.

You might ask me what was I doing this whole time. Well, I became a classical philologist, I wrote a work on the *Cleitophon* that has never been published (I still have it among my papers), and then I did an examination essay on Pindar, and for about three years I did nothing at all nothing. Actually, I was doing nothing but this Jaeger critique, which I did on the basis my knowledge of classical philology.

D.: So the meaning of this entire effort was that you freed yourself from the problem of the ontological conception of value or, at least, from the value ontology of Nikolai Hartmann?

G.: Yes, I would say that!

D.: If we look at Plato and Aristotle, then your critique is simply that Aristotle developed the question of the *agathon,* the good, not on the basis of his critique of the doctrine of ideas, but on the basis of *phronesis.* On the other hand, should the *agathon* in Plato likewise be seen, not on the basis of an ontological perspective, but rather as a question of the ethical (in the genuine sense of the word), hence as a question of dialogue?

G.: Certainly! You're simply posing the question of how my philosophy developed further. Well, I saw both of these things before Heidegger's *Being and Time* appeared, even the critique of the concept of value. From the very first, it had always seemed odd to me that Hartmann could regard the ontology of values as an enhanced form, so to speak, of the concept of realism. And then everything came to me all at once. For a long time, of course, I was working alongside Heidegger and Hartmann constantly — I participated in their seminars, and I even worked on the preparation of their seminar research. The development of Hartmann's ontology and Heidegger's subsequent critique occurred just as I published my first work, which smoothed the way for my academic career.

D.: Summarizing, then, could we say that Nietzsche was correct in his critique of values with respect to every value philosophy where that philosophy is just the flip side of an ontology?

G.: Of course — with respect to a pseudo-objectivism, which seems utterly questionable in relation to a value theory.

D.: So Nietzsche would be correct, and nevertheless the possibility remains open for a future philosophy of finitude, for translating ontology or metaphysics into a philosophy of finitude in exactly the same way that value philosophy is "trans-valued," in Nietzschean terms, into a philosophy of the dialogue.

G.: And this idea was fermenting in Max Scheler as well — in his new ethics, or, more precisely, in his attempt to formulate a new material value ethics. Scheler wrote both of his two books during that time, and he also held lectures in Marburg. Heidegger, however, was always criticizing Scheler. It was only after Heidegger had written *Being and Time* and Scheler had written the first volume of *Formalism in Ethics* that Heidegger's conversion to Scheler took place. Despite his continuing criticism, Heidegger was the only one who understood him.

D.: So this philosophy of finitude has a possibility for the future as well?

G.: Unquestionably. Of course, I always say that I managed to free historicism from its skeptical concrete block, so to speak, by asserting that temporality — finitude   is precisely what the human being is.

D.: And what is positive about this, or what is the positive side of it?

G.: I saw the positive side of it in the relationship to the other, and so I led the dialectic toward the dialogue. Thus the dialectic of an absolutizing (in Hegelian terms) or a skeptical/historicist worldview is translated into the ethical dimension of the dialogue. That was the topic of my habilitation thesis, *Plato's Dialectical Ethics,* which I produced right after my state examination with Heidegger. My state exam went well, even though the examination commission winked at much of it — particularly Friedländer, who thought a great deal of my scholarly abilities and was therefore firmly convinced that I would become a classical philologist. I think I told to you how that went. The state examination came, and Heidegger and Friedländer were both, to a certain extent, at great pains to present me in a good light. I very nearly embarrassed myself because I didn't know enough and I hadn't read much. But Friedländer said to me much later, "Well, you know, I conceived of my task as establishing whether or not you could become a good teacher of Greek. And, when I had established this, I said to the others (honestly), 'He will become a very good teacher.' This is why I gave you a mark of 'good.' I can't say that I would have been very satisfied had we chosen not to speak up for you."

D.: And Heidegger, what did he think?

G.: Heidegger was satisfied with the discussion. He gave me a mark of "with distinction," the highest evaluation. In any case, that was what the whole thing was like. I was allowed through, even though the recording secretary, a *Gymnasium* headmaster, was extraordinarily dissatisfied because there was so much that I didn't know. "You should have known that," he often said, or something similar. It was very unpleasant. So those were his complaints, and I was accepted. And the Latin essay on Pindar, which Glenn Most now wants to republish, was quite good. It has been found again, and he wants to publish it no matter what because he is very impressed by it. Primarily, he tells me, because it is a wonderful piece of Latin, and then just because it is a good essay. Although I said to him, "Listen, it isn't worth it." I have no reason to be ashamed of it, but I find it quite dated — it's been already seventy years since I wrote it. But he wants to print it in Latin and German along with Pindar's Greek text. Such, then, were the requirements of the habilitation. And it so happened that, after the examination, Friedländer and Heidegger went home together, and Friedländer said to Heidegger that evening, "I want to habilitate him!"[1] The next morning I got a letter — I still remember it very clearly. Heidegger asked me over to the house. He had a hoarse voice. He was a little sick, lying on the sofa, and he said I should tell him what I wanted to do. So I told him, and he addressed me informally for the first time. I later realized what he wanted — he wanted to habilitate me. He had thought it all out in advance. He knew from Natorp that he would soon be going to Freiburg. He was thinking, "That's what's in store for me soon," and so he said to me, "You shouldn't be in a hurry. I would very much like to habilitate you." "In the meantime," he urged me, "show them what you can do." The fact that I had learned a great deal really came out in the seminars. I was something of a crutch for him, as much for reading Aristotle as for reading Plato, though mainly for Plato, because, right

---

1. [That is to say, Friedländer wanted to supervise Gadamer's qualifying to become a university professor.]

up to his death, he rebuked me for traveling to America instead of writing my book on Plato. He later realized that he wasn't entitled to rebuke me for this, because it was through me that he saw that he had been wrong to think about Plato's relationship to Aristotle as he did.

D.: So, to come back to the topic of the philosophy of finitude, your habilitation thesis would show that the philosophy of finitude must be understood in terms of this ethical turn, that is, you came to the principle of translating ethics into an ethics of the dialogue. Is there also a possibility that the philosophy of finitude leads us out of the blind alley of historical relativism? You once said of Heidegger that he showed us that we get beyond historicism precisely by recognizing our finitude. Would that mean that the possibility of an ontology of historicity lies precisely in our finitude?

G.: Yes — that was then the meaning of our encounter with Hegel. This is where the essays in *Hegel's Dialectic* (which you yourself translated) come from. All of this came out of the time I was holding lectures in Leipzig. I was reading a great deal about Kant and Fichte and Schelling and Heidegger and, most of all, Hegel. All of it emerged during this period, after I had developed my idea about Plato's dialectic being an ethical thesis. Of course, from the standpoint of the philosophy of finitude, it's possible for us to acquire historical consciousness again without falling prey to historical relativism, exactly to the extent that we recognize the limits of all knowledge, which is bounded precisely by it own historical situation. This recognition gives us back the possibility of seeing the past from our historical perspective, a possibility that I called the "fusion of horizons." Yet the meaning of our finitude doesn't exhaust itself in this alone. What I had already tried to show Heidegger in Marburg and later developed further in the Lisbon lecture and in other essays was, as I have already said, that the genuine meaning of our finitude or our "thrownness" consists in the fact that we become aware, not only of our being historically conditioned, but especially of our being conditioned by the other. Precisely in our ethical relation to the other, it becomes clear to us how difficult it is to do justice to the demands of the other or even simply to become aware of them. The only way not to succumb to our finitude is to open ourselves to the other, to listen to the "thou" who stands before us.

2
Ethics or Metaphysics

D.: We might now pose a second question so as to steer this theme of the philosophy of finitude toward a conclusion: Couldn't we say that this reflection on Plato freely allows us to pursue a different possibility — the metaphysical question? Do you think that dialogical philosophy actually opens new possibilities in this direction?

G.: Yes. Certainly.

D.: To what extent?

G.: It would extend to history, along with being, and perhaps the schema of "being and value-being" [*Sein und Wert-sein*]. With Hartmann I learned that we do find categories in Kant, but we also find values. The difference is that the categories determine the things themselves; the values determine only our mode of being. That had never been made clear to me. Now, you have to understand that you should no longer separate being and being-good, as it were. This is why I later decided to invoke the maxim of not speaking of *Dasein,* but rather of the "Da." This means that the "Da" is there [*das "Da" da ist*], and this results in a further concretizing of the "Da," so it means that the "Da" takes the place of the subject. I think I understood this then, and this is why some of the things that I later developed were now becoming clear to me. You have to look at the essay from the seventh volume of my collected works entitled "The Idea of the Good in Plato and Aristotle," which details a fruitful presupposition about the good, because I say there that you can't distinguish between them — you don't have being *and* the good; the two are inseparable. And, as far as that goes, there isn't a metaphysics of being on the one hand and a moral philosophy on the other. The two are inseparable.

D.: So both moments, being and value, are also contained in it?

G.: Precisely. And the two being together meant that this was where I had the greatest possibility of detaching myself from metaphysics — because both questions should be posed together. Only then is a metaphysics in order in that it shouldn't simply be dissolved; it should be carried back into the ethical question instead.

D.: So we could say that ethics is not simply the "Second Science," as opposed to the "First Science," which, for Aristotle, is metaphysics, but that metaphysics is legitimized as an inner moment within the ethical question. That is, mere "being" and the meaning of this being as "being-in-the-world" or as originary temporality doesn't interest us; being only interests us insofar as it stands in relation to our "Da." It wasn't so much Heidegger who really develop this as it was Nietzsche — existence as perspective, that is, or being in a perspective. In their thinking, perspective would be the moment of the "Da" in *Dasein* that integrates ethical and metaphysical being. So, within this perspective of the "Da" stands the basic principle of a philosophy of interpretation, that is, a hermeneutic philosophy — if hermeneutics is not supposed to be just a method of reading texts but a philosophy?

G.: Yes, most definitely.

D.: At this point, I think, we could take up the question of the various Plato interpretations — those of the Tübingen school and the Milan school, which have recently become affiliated. How should one read the doctrine of the good in Plato's *Republic*? As a metaphysics, as an ethics, or as a politics?

G.: This is indeed a genuine question, and it is hardly possible for me to give a different response to it from the one I have already indicated, because we generally don't find the character of the concepts in the *Republic* to be definitive, whether it be the concept of being or the concept of value or the good. For me, the definitive thing is that both concepts always signify a beyond, a transcendence. Hence what is entirely clear in the *Politeia* — that is, that the sun is beyond being, and the sun, of course, is just a symbol for the indefinability of the good. For the composition of the *Politeia* is such that the virtues are dealt with and defined first, and, having done that, the text then prepares to deal with the good for the first time. But Socrates immediately responds by saying, "I can't do this by myself." And so we get the analogy of the sun, which is just a metaphor for saying that one can't look directly at the good just as one can't look directly at the sun —

even though everything becomes good by means of the good just as everything is illuminated by means of the sun. This analogy with the sun is all one can say about the good as the "beyond" of being.

D.: Now we can bring the *Politeia* into connection with the *Philebus.* Don't you think that the treatment of the good in the *Republic* can be related to the way in which the problem of happiness is treated in the *Philebus,* that is, that it can be related to the concept of the right measure and the right mean? And don't you think that one can relate this concept of the right measure, that is, of the correct relationship between the quality and the quantity of pleasure, between pleasure and knowledge, to the Aristotelian concept of *prepon,* the excellent, the obligatory? Do you think this is just a way out of the problem of the indefinability of the good, or is it not perhaps a productive way to make some headway with the problem of the good without falling back into a value ontology?

G.: The *Philebus.* Well, the question is dealt with so strangely there. If one thinks in a sufficiently hermeneutical way, then I would say that it's no cause for concern; for this, too, is really just an indication of something — namely, once again, that there is an inseparability between what is theoretically important and the good.

D.: On the other hand, of course, we must say that the interpretations of the Tübingen school and the Milan school go in an entirely different direction — especially Joachim Krämer. In both the doctrine of the right measure in the *Philebus* and the doctrine of right mean in the *Politics,* he finds a principle for recognizing not just being but value as well. Then, once again, through an interpretation of Plato's unwritten doctrine, he finds it possible to determine the types from the perspective of the good. Furthermore, by interpreting the dialectic as *dihairesis,* that is, as a doctrine of the classification of types from the highest to the lowest and through the inverse movement (from the lowest kind to the highest), they arrive at the indivisible type, that is, they find the possibility of arriving at the good as the ultimate ground of being, knowing, and willing. They claim, in essence, that the doctrine of the good is an ontology, and the dialectic is the ultimate foundation for ontology and the ultimate end of value ontology. For them, the good is of the highest type, as is the principle of the harmony of the three parts of the soul and the three castes of the *polis,* of the state; ontology, that is, becomes an ethics and constitutes the basis of politics. The mixture of the types in the *Philebus*, where the good becomes the principle of order, harmony, and the correct mixture that leads to happiness, are interpreted in these same terms. On the other hand, hermeneutic philosophy and its interpretation of the dialectic point in a different direction. But where does the difference lie if, as you say, one cannot separate being from the good? Is it possible to make the inseparability of being and value fruitful for an ethics without falling back into an ontology? Or must we admit with the Tübingen philosophers that Plato's unwritten doctrine actually brings us to the knowledge of the good and that, consequently, the dialectic gives us this knowledge?

G.: You see, they treat human beings like gods. If it were possible, through the dialectic, for me to come to knowledge of the good as the ultimate ground of being, then I would be God.

D.: Then what is the proper relationship between dialectic and ontology, between being and the good? And what is the role of the dialectic in relation to ethics and politics? Do you also relate the *prepon* to the correct mean in the *Politics?* Or do you perhaps have a different interpretation of it?

G.: Yes, of course, I have a different interpretation. The *prepon,* once again, is actually something that one can only determine *in concreto,* in the respective situation. This is the only adequate description of the *prepon.* It is actually something that cannot be deduced. Any explication of the good with regard to its content is wrong in principle. The good is not a being in this sense — it is not a highest type. This is really stated quite clearly. I am still pondering how their interpretation is meant to be justified. First come the various virtues, and then a completely new dimension is achieved with the *agathon* — and yet it isn't simply a further *arete,* a further virtue; it is now what is common to all as a new perspective.

D.: But what is this new perspective for? Doesn't it serve to determine the harmonies of the three parts of the soul and thereby to organize the *polis?* The city, of course, is the soul writ large, and there are just three classes in the *polis,* three social castes that correspond to the parts of the soul. In the *polis,* we can see better how one can harmonize the three parts of the soul. This harmony of the soul is disclosed to us through the idea of the good so that, in the light of this idea, we know not only how we have to educate our souls but

also how we should govern our city. That's precisely the point of
the vision of the idea of the good, which is also the principle of the
Politeia and, therefore, of politics.

G.: That's all too difficult for me to understand. I mean, it's surely
nonsense to be believe that human beings are like gods. Yet those
are presuppositions that are chiseled into the text and into Krämer's
thinking, and they are simply wrong. In my opinion, neither Plato
nor Aristotle thought that.

D.: I would like to know your counter-interpretation. Why is this vision of the *agathon*, the good, present in this passage? Even though it
says the good is *epeikeina tes ousias*, it is still decisive for the *Politeia*.

G.: The *Politeia* is really describing all of the phases of education.
The *Politeia* is not actually about the idea that, in the end, one will
know everything and do everything correctly. The state described in it
is one that is meant to lead to a tyrant not necessarily being a tyrant,
but, instead, approximating himself to what a just citizen is. It is
really a disavowal of the city of Athens and the corrupt Athenian
democracy. Plato's intellectual dialogues are really just objects for
discussion. The idea that a doctrine stands behind them — even a
doctrine that one could write down — is completely denied by the
Seventh Letter. In the long run, the Tübingen school will never gain
general acceptance if they don't give the *Seventh Letter* up.[1] But, then,
I would bring all kinds of artillery to bear in its defense. That can't
be why the dialogues are what they are, either. And it isn't just the
Seventh Letter that shows us this; the dialogues show it as well. And
we also see how all of them are really just an inducement, as it were,
to the same kind of thinking. So this situation of the metaphysician
who dwells in the perception of the truth is simply not a human
situation — there is no such thing. This is also the case with *nous*,
divine thinking. I think it was very important [for Aristotle] to stress
this in the *phronesis* section [of the *Nicomachean Ethics*]; this section
is extremely relevant today. For it shows that *phronesis* naturally
contemplates *nous*, which guarantees the particular, on the one hand,
and the universal, on the other.

D.: And then, of course, the question is, "Are the particular and the
universal bound together?"

1. [Presumably because they misinterpret it so badly.]

G.: Yes. I think the *Nicomachean Ethics* is quite explicit about this. *Nous* is both the highest and the lowest at the same time. As I have often reiterated, it seems that *phronesis* is only meant to investigate the means through which the human being is meant to effect the ideal of virtue or the virtuous human being. But it's clear that the knowledge of the means can't leave out of consideration the knowledge of the final end of every action. And this is done on a specific basis (one to which I have always given priority) — that the meaning of every ethical action is never something specific, never a specific deed, an *ergon;* instead, it is simply pure and straightforward *euprattein,* good action. Every investigation into the means, therefore, must have this in it because the search is itself an action directed toward an end. In this sense, the search is simultaneously *logos* (thinking) and *ergon* (acting).

D.: Does occupying oneself with *nous* just mean that one is doing metaphysics, ethics, and politics at the same time?

G.: All of them, yes.

D.: Would *theoria,* in the Greek sense — that is, viewing the universal as participation in *nous* and pursuing it through *phronesis* — also be *praxis?*

G.: Yes, the highest form of *praxis.* That's quite beautiful, a lovely idea. Nevertheless, all of this seems very unfamiliar to me because I live so completely in the conviction that this sense of metaphysics is quite marvelous; and this is why I'll have to look into *De Anima* again, which I did study very closely at one time.

D.: The Tübingen School is also of the opinion that one shouldn't start from the dialogues. But my view is that the dialogues are evidence for the unitary theory that stands behind them. They are an indication that the unwritten doctrine, which one can reconstruct, is an authentic doctrine. Of course, they begin with the *Seventh Letter* as well. And while they don't think the doctrine was ever written down, unlike you, they do conclude that the doctrine was there — as an esoteric doctrine.

G.: Yes, but nevertheless, the *Seventh Letter* strongly emphasizes that there never will be any such theory per se; in each case, rather, it will be like a spark that suddenly illuminates us.

D.: This doctrine isn't fixed in writing, but it's there as a theory in the esoteric circles and can be communicated through these verbally.

G.: No. That completely contradicts the *Seventh Letter.* What it says there is that one can gain sudden insight in a conversation by means of this spark that lights up between people who are compelled by good will to come to an agreement.

D.: So, as we are also told in the *Republic,* we will come to a vision of the good through this spark that illuminates us. But then we are supposed to know how to translate it into *praxis,* and wouldn't that, in turn, be a matter of *phronesis*?

G.: *Nous* is really the same thing as both of these. And this chapter of the *Nicomachean Ethics* shows quite well how the universal, just as much as the concrete, is always *nous.* This doesn't seem at all consistent with any kind of theory, be it a doctrine or a metaphysics. There is *nous,* of course, but that certainly doesn't mean that an existence follows from it; it's something that must always be there with our thinking and must always lead us in the conversation.

D.: Is this how it is with the *agathon* as well, with the good?

G.: The *agathon* is also a final end of this kind, yes. It's an expression for this thing that is never quite attainable. I think it is precisely what justifies hermeneutics. Actually, one always sees it as a transcending of what one already thinks one knows. I readily admit that Aristotle also presented it a bit like this — as if there were a "Da"; but, then, he sometimes criticizes it.

D.: He criticizes the idea of the good, but he does act as if this *nous* existed. It must be *energeia,* the highest form of *energeia,* the highest reality. It's also referred to as *entelecheia,* which means action that has its purpose in itself. Is this *entelecheia* also an expression of the divine?

G.: Certainly, the divine is *entelecheia,* but whether or not the divine exists isn't really the point here. In any case, for the human being it's the beyond.

D.: Is the *agathon* in Plato the same thing — the "beyond" of being, that is?

G.: Yes, yes. I think it is all quite integrated. This is why I would say that one must dispense with this contrast between being and the good. I would simply say that the good is transcendence or the beyond. No one can say whether it is or is not, whether it has being or whether it is beyond being. This question is posed on an entirely different basis, an entirely different level from that of our field of experience where we can demonstrate existence. It is precisely a question of transcendence, and that means that the world of our experience is transcended in the idea of the good. But it also means that our world is oriented toward the good and comes to completeness in it without our being able to understand or prove with the objects of our experience how this happens.

D.: That would be genuine transcendence in your terms, which, in this respect, is connected to the finitude of worldly things (as Heidegger understood it), and for which the finitude of our understanding directly entails a transcending of our experience.

G.: Yes, certainly.

D.: If, as Plato would have it, we can now grasp the idea of the good only through this good that suddenly illuminates us, then, of course, the big question poses itself: When we are confronted with problems of *praxis* and attempt to put this illumination into practice, how can this spark give us positive insights for our conduct? Can our behavior really be guided by the idea of the good?

G.: We know that in Plato the good is the highest fulfillment and completion of being. And if we strive in our actions toward this fulfillment of being, as Book IX of the *Republic* commends us to do, and we can experience this fulfillment, then we know that we have acted according to this spark. But it looks like we only know after the fact that this fulfillment of life came from our having acted according to this vision of the good, whereas we thought we were acting according to our *phronesis,* and we thought we had developed our practical knowledge through our rationality. In the end, we are seized by this feeling of fulfillment, and yet only later do we realize that we have acted according to the good. In fact, one can say this for the beautiful as well as the good. So, right away I have something new to work with — the *Symposium* and the speech of Diotima. "You will certainly never catch on to this," she says to Socrates, "now I will lead you forth." That's the Tübingen doctrine — "You will never catch on to this." (Gadamer laughs ironically.) In other words, it isn't a question of a doctrine that can be understood. It isn't a question of a transcendence of the good like the transcendence of God. No, that's really a surreptitious Christianity, which is then reinterpreted back into antiquity.

D.: And perhaps it's not just a surreptitious Christianity but — especially in Krämer's case — a piece of Thomistic ontology that is being projected back into Plato.

G.: Yes, certainly.

D.: Would you follow Nietzsche's interpretation, then, according to which Christianity is a kind of Platonism for the masses?

G.: No, no. If I said Christianity just now, I really meant to say, "a theological Christianity." The situation is repeated in theology in exactly the same way — a piece of contemporary theology is projected back into the ancient world. Real Christianity is something other than theological Christianity. I mean Christianity as genuine faith and life *praxis*. This is the Christianity that maintains itself in spite of everything, as we have seen, for example, in Russia. But this Christianity is something other than the theological.

D.: Doesn't the discourse of life *praxis* refer us to a close connection among religion, ethics, and politics — not in the sense of our European history as the history of Christianity, but rather in the genuine sense (which you perhaps also intend) according to which our openness and our commitment to the other entail not only the intuitive grasp of our own finitude but also a fulfillment that is very similar to religious enthusiasm (in the Greek sense of "being in God")?

G.: Yes, I do believe this. Yet the question of finitude is much more powerful than one thinks. I can't really understand what the Tübingen school is trying to do. The Greeks conceived of the gods with complete awareness — but as the other. They really didn't conceive of a unity in the godhead. There are several hints of this kind, but on the whole . . . (Gadamer shakes his head skeptically) . . . I think that in another fifty years — in the event that there still is a European civilization by then — those of us who wish to understand it should try to work out the meaning of the Gnostic question or the question of the neo-Platonists. I think it was Plotinus who was supposed to have thought about a feeling of oneness with being as a whole.

So I have never sufficiently reconciled myself with the Tübingen school because it seemed clear to me that this is simply an Aristotelian question that can only be posed for the sake of argument. The doctrine is not as important to me, but I quite confidently expect to understand the questions.

3

Utilitarianism, Pragmatism, Pluralism (Calogero, Rorty, Popper)

D.: Having now clarified the meaning of transcendence as well as the religious dimension to which human finitude belongs, and after you have also suggested the difference between Greek and Christian religiosity, we can now return again to the problem of the good and ask about it once again from an ethical and political standpoint. Don't you think that Plato himself looks upon the good as a real principle of ethical and political life? Insofar as he polemicizes against the Sophists (who reclaim the good as a supreme principle of life *praxis* and wish to defend it as that which is simply useful), doesn't Plato have a better criterion for public life? That is, wasn't the *Politeia* about Plato showing us that in political life it's not merely a question of doing things according to utility but rather of following the good or arriving at the good? Couldn't the constant polemic against the Sophists bring us directly to the notion that Plato wanted to derive positive criteria for political life from the idea of the good?

G.: Once again, this whole discourse strikes me as a little comical. Just what should we expect in the *Politeia,* in the *Republic*? A sketch is drawn of an ideal city of which it is said — quite plainly — that it cannot exist, that it cannot be realized; there's no doubt about this. For example, when the text speaks of education, it says that everyone older than eight years old should be expelled from the city because they can no longer be educated. How can one found a city if all of the people are supposed to be under the age of eight? So, we aren't dealing with a plan for actually founding a city or a real civic entity, but, as I said, we are dealing instead with an indirect critique of

the Athenian democracy (which could no longer be governed demo-
cratically) through the presentation of its counter-example — as in a
Jonathan Swift satire.

The principle that declares that parents aren't supposed to know
their children and that the city is one single family where the children
are meant to recognize all of the guardians as their fathers should be
understood as a counter-example as well. It definitely should not be
understood as a real principle of life *praxis*; instead, it's merely in-
tended to give Athenian families to understand that their city can
go to ruin if they persist in wanting to put only their own children forward as city leaders. All of this indicates that we are not
dealing here with any real civic doctrine or any real principles of genuine political life (and rather less with a civic doctrine) — doctrines
and principles, that is, that are deduced from a supreme principle
(from the good) in such a way that the philosopher could have a
principle for founding a state at his disposal simply by knowing
this supreme principle. The *Seventh Letter* tells us quite explicitly
that Plato would never have written such a doctrine or considered
such a doctrine to be possible. But because it was inconvenient for
them people later began to say that the *Seventh Letter* couldn't be
genuine.

D.: So, as you have already written in your essay "Dialectic and
Sophism in Plato's Seventh Letter," one cannot distinguish the philosopher from the Sophist?

G.: Of course, one cannot distinguish him from the Sophist, and
neither can one distinguish oneself from him unless one is precisely
an *other*.

D.: And how is one precisely an other?

G.: Only by not thinking one knows what one doesn't know. The
Socratic profession of ignorance or "knowledge of ignorance" is the
decisive thing — if it's actually meant and practiced. In opposition to
the whole of Sophism, Socrates always maintained that knowledge
of the just and unjust and, ultimately, knowledge of the good could
never be the object of a particular *techne*, that is, a particular kind of
knowing that exhausts itself (unlike every other kind of knowing) in
the knowledge of the rules according to which one produces something. On the contrary, practical knowing — that is, knowing about

what is just and unjust — is a different kind of knowing, which, according to Socrates, appears first as a form of not-knowing and as the soul's constant search for the just and unjust. This was regarded, above all, as a kind of resistance to those who would rather teach the art of justice as the highest form of state utility.

D.: So, in relation to simple not-knowing, couldn't we find a more positive criterion that says that the philosopher is in search of dialogue and attempts to engage others in dialogue and to understand and to respect them by means of the dialogue, whereas the Sophist simply wants to persuade the other of what he has in mind and of what he himself wants from the other?

G.: That distinction seems too facile to me. After all, a person who is trying to persuade isn't trying to compel the other but to reach a consensus with him.

D.: Then let's take into consideration the nobler criticism that Plato levies against Protagoras in the *Theatetus* as he puts the self-defense of Protagoras into the mouth of Socrates. Here Protagoras himself explains that he never tries to persuade the other of what is true or false, for no one has really been able to do this, and no one ever will. In a discussion no one will admit that he intends something false or that he has been wrong. But that's not what is at issue in the discussion. On the other contrary, Protagoras just wants to convince the other of what would be better — to convince the city of what would be a better constitution for them, and a better form of government, as well as a better decision about what would be more useful for the city. This is why he wants neither to discuss the good in itself nor to persuade anyone of this good in itself; he wants, rather, to persuade them only of what would be better for the city or what would be a higher form of government as opposed to a lower one. This better form is also the one that is more advantageous and more useful for the city. But a person who teaches this on behalf of the city is a just teacher and educator, and this is why it's also just for him to be paid by the city or by its citizens — precisely because he is imparting something more useful. We could look at this self-defense of Protagoras in the *Theatetus* — which Plato even puts into the mouth of Socrates — as the first elaboration of a pragmatic position that's being accepted and defended once again today by Richard Rorty. Politics isn't a question of the good in itself but of the better. It's a process, therefore, of bettering the forms of institutions and classes and of making the correct decisions about these things. So, does Protagoras have it right, as Rorty thinks he does?

G.: Yes, the way things are now this is perhaps the case, and yet, even if it goes unsaid, the tendency to ascribe this betterment process to the priests is very great. This is why I understand Rorty quite well — he actually says that this can't be what Plato intends

D.: No. Rorty doesn't want to differentiate himself from this position at all — he simply means that Protagoras is right in the case of this particular speech in the *Theatetus*. He thinks that politics — that is, the life *praxis* of the *polis* — is precisely not a matter of the true or the good in themselves. After all, in his self-defense (as Socrates expresses it), Protagoras often repeats that one cannot persuade the other of what is true or false, but only of what is more useful to him or of what is better for him. So one can only inform a city of more advantageous laws or a better way of life, and one can persuade its citizens only of what is better — always the better and never the good.

G.: Yes, the good . . . I think Plato essentially wants to say that there can't be any knowledge of the better without a knowledge of the good or without us keeping our eyes open for the good. The polemic against the Sophists has only one meaning — to show that they couldn't have any real knowledge of the better because they established their foothold on the knowledge of the useful, which seemed precisely to be the immediate utility of the city. But that happened only because they didn't have a correct understanding of the good, which, on the contrary, constitutes the *basis* for what is genuinely useful, the general advantage of the state.

D.: If we now look back again to Protagoras and Rorty, can we conclude from this that we can't persuade anyone of what the good is in itself but only of what is better for him? Thus we could never persuade the other of what is true? This is also why Rorty thinks that philosophy has nothing to say in politics if it asks only about the true, because in politics one asks only about the better without being concerned with the true and the good in themselves. Who, after all, could ever arrive at knowledge of the true or the good in itself?

G.: I would perhaps agree with him in that in our search for the good we will, at best, hit upon the better, never the good in itself.

And yet... it's also true that we will never search for or find what is better for us without seeking the good in itself or at least having it in mind.

D.: But doesn't this relationship to the good also have to do with the true? Herein, of course, lies the difficulty.

G.: Naturally — I do understand that this is where the difficulty lies. This is precisely why I say that the difficulty lies not in our not knowing the truth, or the politician not knowing the truth, or his not needing to know the truth. Here Rorty is correct — anyone who engages in politics can't simply desire the true or the good exactly — it's undoubtedly correct to say that he orients his own action and conduct with a view to the pragmatic. One can't simply dispense with what the good politician would have or should have been able to understand, or what he has personally been able to observe in the practical situation. On the contrary, we see that this farsighted discernment of the politician is very often what is decisive in life *praxis* — much like it is with the businessman. I can cite for you the example of Dr. Heinz Götze, who, after the war, immediately saw what was going on here in Heidelberg for what it was — a lack of initiative. There was nothing going on in Heidelberg at the time, and he understood the need for initiative and seized it immediately. He risked a great deal and created the Springer Publishing House, a huge enterprise that now has worldwide significance. All of this, of course, is admirable, and I would say that there is *phronesis* to be found in it as well. If we now return to Rorty, then, we see that he pleads well for this practical or pragmatic reasonableness. If in doing this, however, he limits himself to just this — without referring it back to the good — then he won't be able to recognize what the better is in relation to the good, that is, what the better actually is. One really must recognize that the better is actually only the better in relation to a final end.

D.: Would this be also the reason why philosophy, for him, has nothing to with politics and, conversely, why politics has nothing to do with philosophy?

G.: Yes, just so.

D.: Do you, on the other hand, think that philosophy does have something to do with politics?

G.: Yes, I really do believe that, in certain way, we all engage in politics. By virtue of the fact that we live, after all, in a society and in a state, we can't help doing politics — we have to admit this to ourselves. This is why we also have to pay attention to the rights of others.

D.: To what extent must we admit to ourselves that we engage in politics?

G.: To the extent that we recognize that our actions are always purposeful. And if a person wants to achieve a purpose, then he or she must also persuade others of it and, moreover, gain their consensus. Nevertheless, we have to be clear about whether we want to persuade others because we think it would be something good or whether we simply want to persuade them because it suits our purposes — without even asking whether this would be anything good. What I want to show is that, whether we can answer it or not, we should always begin from the idea of posing the question of the *agathon,* the good. The question is always whether it's simply a matter of what's better or whether it is really a matter of what lies beyond every particular purpose.

D.: Here, again, we come upon the old question of how to relate the good to the better and vice versa. This, in my opinion, would be the reason why philosophy would still have something to do with politics; and yet here, once again, we hit upon the greatest difficulty: Who can know what the good is in itself?

G.: Yes, indeed; and here I would agree with Rorty again. I admit that when we search for the good we can, at most, perhaps find the better. I think that we can only recognize the good in the way that Socrates speaks of in the *Symposium* — the good, in other words, is the beautiful. And this, says Diotima, Socrates will not understand, because, knowing him, he will remain completely speechless before the beautiful. He doesn't want to hear anything else, because what he sees suffices for him completely. This is what happens in the beautiful — in becoming manifest in the beautiful the good relativizes itself.

D.: Does this mean that it has become aesthetically manifest?

G.: One can describe it in aesthetic terms. But, of course, it isn't just that. That's one possibility, one way in which it presents itself and appears to us.

D.: And would that be why it appears to us at the end of the *Philebus,* or at the conclusion of the *Politeia,* and also in the *Seventh Letter?*

G.: Of course, and it seems to me to have an inner coherence and necessity. In the end, if you assume that he wants to be able to prove everything, one can only wonder whether Plato himself isn't ultimately subject to his own burden of proof. This is precisely the point at which he leaves me unsatisfied. We have the same thing in Aristotle's case with his final principle of motion, which turns into the idea of a prime unmoved mover.

D.: Could we say then that insofar as Plato and Aristotle want to refer everything back to a final purpose, be it Plato's idea of the good or Aristotle's unmoved mover as *entelecheia* (final purpose), this is precisely where their ideas come into agreement?

G.: You see, this idea of a prime mover is exactly what doesn't convince me in Aristotle. An idea is introduced directly into the supporting argument here that, in my opinion, doesn't belong.

D.: You mean the idea of the prime mover, which really should remain unmoved, being the principle of movement or self-movement?

G.: It's the transition to this concept that I find very weak — as it is carried out in Book Lambda of the *Metaphysics.* Initially, Aristotle is dealing here with the meaning of analogy, and then, all of a sudden, the idea of the prime mover or the unconditioned mover is introduced. The way he introduces this concept here has always seemed odd to me. That is, here we have the introductory chapter on analogy (which stems from the fruits of Academic thought), and then suddenly this leap — a leap into a concept from which he cannot escape and one that I can (perhaps) only understand as his originary conception of the living being.

D.: In that case, could we say that this conception of the living being as originary self-movement — *autokinoun* — is identical with the concept of the good in Plato's *Politeia?*

G.: Certainly, and this is precisely why I think that Plato and Aristotle are not so far apart from one another. Even the way in which Aristotle establishes his system of astronomy seems to me to be a refined way of positioning himself on the opposite side of what is universal/provable. The will to prove everything has, as they say, two sides.

D.: Here we hit upon another very important problem, the problem, that is, of the relationship between rhetoric and hermeneutics. How is the relationship to the thou that takes place in dialogue to be conceived from your hermeneutic position? Is it possible to persuade the other of the truth, or can we only persuade him of what is true for me alone, that is to say, of "my truth," just as the other is persuaded only of his truth? Or should we not say that I can persuade the other, but, at the same time, I must presuppose that he can also persuade me of what he holds to be true? Or should the I-and-thou relationship be conceived quite differently — that is, is there an objective criterion according to which one can decide upon the true and the false?

G.: I always imagined the matter like this — when we engage in a dialogue, what I think or what the other thinks is completely relative to that moment when, all of a sudden, a spark suspends [*aufhebt*] a misunderstanding and makes possible a clear acceptance of what becomes visible in that instant. After all, it seems to me that the difference doesn't really relate to the question of a preconceived set of rules at all; for it is obviously true that we human beings always have only limited horizons. On the whole, this strikes me as quite healthy for dogmatists, but I really can't believe that with this kind of pragmatism one can dispense with the fact that one person sees some things as being more important than the other one does. I know about Rorty . . . yes indeed — and if we want to take a few steps, Rorty gets us there quite well, but when it comes to consequences like these, I can no longer quite see it. In any event, I think the difference between God and the human being remains an absolute one, and we must therefore recognize this without arriving at an absolute criterion for truth that could be only a divine criterion.

D.: Having come this far, we should point out that this difference and this relation to the absolute as transcendence plays no role for Rorty. This was also true for Guido Calogero in Italy. For him, it was a question of his status as a layman — that is, of an argument that he directed against the priests, as you put it, and not against Christianity per se. Many years ago, in the fifties, when Calogero wanted to pose the question of dialogue in Italian culture and politics forcefully, he formulated the issue like this: If I begin a dialogue with someone — if it is meant to be a genuine dialogue — then I must presuppose that the other could also be right. I must therefore place my own conviction in brackets. This was the foundation of his doctrine of the dialogue, which he laid out in his then famous book, *Logo e dialogo*. We do not enter into a dialogue on the basis of the truth of our convictions or our ethical principles, but on the basis of our sheer will to dialogue, that is, on the basis of our respect and recognition of the other. Here, there is no longer any relationship to transcendence — it no longer plays any role. Is this the case for you as well?

G.: No. I am very dissatisfied with this. By putting it this way, he avoids the question of whether one is right and the other is wrong. I don't really see it that way. I also find it definitively correct to say that the Sophist is not the Sophist because he constantly has new arguments for his theses. This is certainly not it. If I may express it with an example — in a particular instance I could ask myself, "Have I done the right thing?" — which I acknowledge after the fact — or, "Have I not done the right thing?" What I have done in each instance is just as true — it all happened in exactly the same way. But it's not simply a question of the bare truth — whether or not I did this or that; instead, it's a question of the way in which I can explain the action — that is, whether or not I did something right in the sense of something just, something that I can justify to myself and to the other. We can always try, of course, to give an answer in either the first way or in the second; but subsequently we become aware that it's not simply a question of the sheer truth but of whether or not we can justify and take responsibility for our actions. This is what Protagoras wants to distinguish in his argument — it's not a question of the sheer truth but of what is better or not. So it's really a question of what is just and what is unjust. It's correct to say that one cannot distinguish the Sophist from the philosopher through mere speech. But the difference is precisely that it's not just about the truth of the speech!

D.: Do you mean to say that in the case of the Sophist and in that of the philosopher we are always seeking something different through our discourse?

G.: How so?

D.: Does the Sophist seek only to persuade the other of what is better for him, and does the philosopher, on the other hand, seek only the truth?

G.: Yes, of course, I did understand what you meant. But I'm trying to hold fast to this distinction by saying that there are obviously always limitations — we are never gods. But, in spite of this, it does make a difference whether what one says (for my own knowledge is never completely certain either) is the same thing as what the Sophist says. The Sophist makes things quite convenient for himself, convenient for his own particular purposes. This is why I don't really believe that this is a very strong position — though I readily admit that it has a high critical value to it. On the other hand, people who imagine themselves to be in possession of actual absolute truth, truth that has gained acceptance through uncritical choice, still give preference to those who maintain a critical-pragmatic position. Nevertheless, I would say that the right answer is to say that, even with pragmatic intentions, one cannot generally distinguish the Sophist from the philosopher. Indeed, the difference, or the differentiating, is not a matter of definition. It may be that we have the possibility, as pure observers, to distinguish between what could be right or wrong. But, in truth, the question of what we do right or what we do wrong is what genuinely concerns us. As Plato has Protagoras express it in exactly the passage that you cited, the basic principle that Socrates himself is supposed to maintain with respect to this is to commit no *adikia,* no injustice, in our discourse with one another. One does, however, commit an injustice in questioning and answering or in refutation when one desires only to argue and win with no regard for the reasoning of the other.

D.: Let's return now to Calogero and his position, which we can also characterize as a pluralistic one or a position of highest dialogical openness. We are, he says, in one continuous dialogue with the other, or we live in a dialogue....

G.: Yes, we live constantly in dialogue — we could even say that we are a living dialogue....

D.: If we now maintain ourselves in this position of complete openness with respect to the other, then we are also prepared to be persuaded by him about what he considers correct, just as we would like to persuade him of what we consider to be correct. If we maintain this position, then, don't all our possible points of view about what is right or wrong or, better, about what is just or unjust, have the same significance or the same validity?

G.: I wouldn't say that at all. If I declare myself ready to enter into a dialogue with the other, then, presumably, I cannot be of the same opinion with him, or, rather, I can intend something different from what the other thinks. And, indeed, in the majority of cases this is just how it is — I intend something different, or I think differently from him. The desire to persuade someone is not a renunciation of the truth as such. Rather, if I hold something to be true, then I try to persuade the other of it — but the presupposition for this is that I do hold something to be true. The Sophist who completely denies this loses precisely that basis that is the real basis of dialogue.

D.: To "enter into" dialogue, then, does not mean to renounce the truth claim of my opinion or any truth claim, as Calogero would have it, or as a contemporary pluralistic point of view that advocates the highest dialogical openness would have it.

G.: No, not at all. On the contrary, it presupposes this truth claim, be it my truth or his. For if I also admit that the other can persuade me, what is it that he is supposed to be persuading me of if not what is true?! Of course, I value Calogero's pluralistic position very much, just as I appreciate his early essays on ancient philosophy, particularly the ones on the Eleatics. I have his essays here (Gadamer points to the bookcase on the wall). I also knew him quite well, personally. Unfortunately, I didn't manage to bring him to Heidelberg. I invited him often — even on behalf of the Hegel Society — and I also wrote him a personal letter in an effort to persuade him, but he always refused.

Now, the pluralistic position isn't simply Protagoras' position, which you brought up in connection with Rorty's Neo-pragmatism. But it seems that the position of pluralism, precisely as it was formulated by Calogero, leads to an *epoche,* a Husserlian withholding of judgment that hardly seems tenable to me. In the first place, it dispenses with the basic presupposition of the dialogue, namely, the presupposition of the truth claim; and, second, like the Husserlian *epoche,* it dispenses with any historical horizon, and it thus becomes somewhat realistically and historically incomprehensible and untenable. We are all historically conditioned, and our effective-historical consciousness contains a truth claim (which I have also referred to as "the anticipation of the completeness") toward which we all strive, even if we will never reach it.

D.: But there is also another kind of Sophist — one who appears quite different from the Protagoras depicted by Plato in the *Theatetus* and who doesn't correspond to Rorty's pragmatic position either. This is that other Sophist that Plato has in mind and with whom he always has Socrates engaged in polemic. It's the ordinary Sophist, the one who sees dialogue only as a platform for his art and speech, only as a means of seizing power. His sole purpose is to exact consensus or to persuade surreptitiously. In contrast to the pluralistic position, he presents the position of naked utilitarianism. Anyone who wields the power of speech as the power of persuasion can employ this power for his own purposes. And, furthermore, anyone who develops an art from this and acquires this art can sell it for a great deal of money, especially to the sons of the rich and powerful, who consequently learn to exact a consensus from society and thereby have their own agendas adopted in the city. This is the later Sophism that Plato depicts at the beginning of the *Republic* in the figure of Thrasymachus, according to whom justice is merely the advantage of the stronger. Isn't there a real danger in this art of speech, this rhetoric that was promulgated mainly by the Sophists? You, on the other hand, seem to value this art highly as a necessary presupposition of genuine communication and even the critique of ideology.

G.: Well, in this case I would say that we're really looking at something different. I have obviously thought a great deal about rhetoric as well. One can consider rhetoric from two sides. On the one hand, one can see it from the negative perspective that you just formulated — as the art of being able to prove everything and its opposite, that is, as the practice of the art of persuasion, while remaining completely silent about the question of truth or what is right. One can, of course, also develop a broader conception of rhetoric — the idea that one can also persuade someone of what is true without being able to prove it. When Gorgias, for instance (who is always cited in this context and to whom you alluded), teaches us how to persuade someone of both a thesis and its antithesis, he is not trying to show that both theses are provable, but rather that the power of persuasion lies in something other than sheer proof. We can conclude from this that the art of persuading is something different from the art of proving, but we can mainly see that one can also persuade someone of what is true (and not merely of what is false) without being able to prove it. So, if Gorgias is always claiming that he knows how bend the power of speech to his service, then this is correct per se, but that doesn't prevent one from calling speech that is not used in this way rhetoric as well — as opposed to the provable. This doesn't have to mean that anything that one can't prove belongs to rhetoric; it means, rather, that rhetoric desires, above all, to persuade us of the true without being able to prove it — therein lies the difference.

D.: Then one can persuade someone of the true without being able to prove it?

G.: Of course. And this does not mean that the proof would be meaningless or that the point is not to prove something. Rhetoric, of course, implies that one wants to persuade someone of what one takes to be true — this is also rhetoric, and this is what we are constantly doing. It's inherent in our speaking with one another and in our mutual understanding.

D.: On the other hand, I think rhetoric for Gorgias consisted in the sheer desire to persuade and in nothing else, thus disregarding the problem of truth. That is to say that Aristotle, in the first book of his *Rhetoric,* says that we are not dealing here with the true but only with the *eikos,* the "veri-similar" [*don Wahr ähnlichen*], and that rhetoric teaches to us how to defend ourselves; for it is unworthy of a human being to be able to defend himself only with the body and not with speech.

G.: No — that wouldn't hold for the Gorgias who is handled with such great respect in Plato. Now, Prodicus and Protagoras — whom we consider to be the precursors of Nietzsche rather than Rorty — they're different. Gorgias, who was a highly gifted man and whose reputation was apparently enormous because he had such enormous eloquence, is respected and praised by Plato because he is reputed to be honest. But, just as we misunderstand Gorgias, we also misunderstand the true sense of Platonic-Aristotelian rhetoric because we remain trapped in a false estimation of rhetoric that we have dragged along with us through the intervening centuries in which the schools of rhetoric have dominated. The rhetoric that we can call the art of speech or persuasion does not, as we have believed for centuries, consist in a body of rules according to whose application and adherence we can achieve victory over our opponent or our partner in public debates or simply in conversation with one another. The art of speech or persuasion consists, rather, in the innate ability —

which we can also, of course, develop and perfect — of being able to actually communicate with others and even persuade them of the true without being able to prove it (assuming that we are no longer able to). It's really a matter of our actually being able to speak to others, and this means that we must appeal to their emotions and their passions (this is why the second book of Aristotle's *Rhetoric* deals with the passions of the human soul), but not in order to deceive others or to profit by it personally, but, instead, to allow what is true to appear and to reveal what we ourselves are persuaded by and what, otherwise (through the usual methods of proof), could not appear as such. This is why Aristotle calls the domain of rhetoric *eikos* — for it is a question of a truth that could appear only in our speech and that otherwise would not be manifest as such. It could even appear as the untrue. There is no absolute guarantee that it would be true, no guarantee of objective proof. But this is what we have before us in the everyday situation of communication, where we do have to defend our *raisons,* our good reasons — not in the sense that we want to foist ourselves on the other, but only in the sense that we should make clear to the other what we believe to be right and what we can show our good reasons for, reasons that are just not as evident to the other person. In order to succeed at this, we need precisely this art of speech or this power of the word. We can now conclude that the philosopher and the Sophist are not to be distinguished sheerly by their argumentation. The mode of arguing is the same, and the difference consists only in the fact that, in the one case, we seek only what is just, and we want to convince the other that it is also what is true; in the other case, we seek only that which appears to us to be more advantageous and more useful. And, in this case, perhaps we also try to make our own advantage appear to be what is just, as long as it can appear (according to the *eikos,* thus *apparently*) to be such a thing.

4

Ethics or Rhetoric (Vico, Nietzsche, Derrida)

D.: Professor Gadamer, after our conversation yesterday about the difference between Sophists and philosophers, we are now far enough along that we can pose the question about the relationship between ethics and rhetoric. The issue seems to be this: When we take Sophism in the pejorative sense that Plato ascribes to it in the *Republic* and in the *Sophist,* then we should say that the ground of the distinction between Sophism and rhetoric can only be an ethical criterion and never a logical one, which is to say, a criterion based on the evidence and verifiability of assertions. If persuasion that leads to a decision depends on an ethical criterion but, at the same time, is meant to be accompanied by arguments that correspond to the logic of proof and (ultimately) the criterion of truth, then the problem arises of how one is supposed to combine these two criteria, which are not equivalent. So which criterion should ultimately determine our decision?

G.: This is precisely the question of *phronesis,* wisdom. But we have to understand that there's something prior to this, and that is rhetoric. Rhetoric is the starting point. The whole of ethics is rhetoric, and the idea that *phronesis* is rhetoric already occurs in Aristotle. *Phronesis* cannot be gauged with a scientific concept like mathematics; it's something quite different — it's rhetoric. He says later that wherever rhetoric is differentiated as such an art, wherever it is not simply a question of the truth (and here he comes relatively close to Plato's *Gorgias*), then rhetoric as such is surely not something bad. It's only bad if it's used badly; then it's something different. Okay, but what is it? Well, we have also been thinking about a completely different side of the human soul — temporality and death — as something that hovers over our lives. I think we must clarify this first, and then we can think about the later accomplishments of Hellenism, Epicureanism, Stoicism, and so on....

D.: But Stoicism has a very pronounced logic — one that's being rediscovered today and greatly admired — a very pronounced rational side....

G.: Yes, certainly, but that's not what is decisive about it. In contrast to this, the Stoics have a phenomenology of human existence that dispenses with and is something quite different from the bare instrumentality of logic. The same tension generally applies to contemporary science. With science we can turn certain forces of nature into instruments. To what extent we can do this and for how long we can do it — that's the problem. Now, in the meantime, of course, it's true that we can really say nothing about this because we realize that what we have understood up to now will no longer suffice in helping humanity reach its goals.

D.: But let's return now to rhetoric. If everything is rhetoric — that is, the desire to persuade and allowing oneself to be persuaded — then, of course, the question becomes this: What place is there left for ethics, that is, for the I-and-thou relationship that Plato also talks so much about?

G.: But obviously there is a place; the place for this relationship is, in fact, *phronesis* — wisdom or reasonableness. *Phronesis,* or reasonableness, is nothing other than the conscious side of action, practical knowing. Whenever we take note of this conscious side of the distinction between I and thou, then we have *phronesis.*

D.: At the beginning of the *Politics,* Aristotle says that we have *logos* not merely when we are discussing the pleasurable and the unpleasurable but also when we are discussing the just and the unjust.

G.: Yes, certainly, but that's later terminology. Right off the bat, of course, you could quite easily object that my whole philosophy is nothing but *phronesis* — but, of course, it *is* nothing but *phronesis,* and this continues to be the case.

D.: But if we carry this so far as no longer to distinguish ethics from rhetoric, then we can no longer distinguish between the discourse that has ethical goals and the discourse that wants only to persuade. But is there no such distinction? That is, don't we have one discourse and a relationship to the other in which we desire only to understand him for the sake of his own interests and another discourse in which we desire only to persuade him for the sake of our own interests? I believe that if we overlook this difference between ethics and rhetoric in order to escape from Sophistic or pragmatic rhetoric, then we are really cheated, because we are left with nothing but sheer persuasion.

G.: But we can't define rhetoric like that. First, think about proof — to define it like that would turn it into an art of proof; but there is no proof in the field of rhetoric. We can't prove anything because it's not mathematics. Even physics is not a strict science, an *episteme*, because it entails *tyche*. One can also define rhetoric in purely negative terms as the art of persuading without being able to prove anything.

D.: It's precisely a matter of the *eikos,* the likely, and in its own domain, therefore, it has nothing to do with truth. One can look at it as the art of the sheer desire to persuade — in contradistinction to ethics, that is — as the art of wanting to have one's own point of view accepted by means of discourse without thinking about the other, who has also put forward his own point of view, his own theses, and his own interests. This respect for the other constitutes precisely the defining feature of genuine dialogue, which is the basis of ethics. Isn't rhetoric, on the other hand, a game of discourse played for the sake of winning a contest with the other?

G.: No, if you look at it that way you'll never be able to understand *synesis* (being reasonable, the understanding of the other as himself), or *syggnome* (that sympathetic insightfulness that inclines toward for-giveness), and so on — everything that one finds in the *Nicomachean Ethics.*

D.: Yes, of course — all of that belongs to ethics and not to rhetoric.

G.: Initially, you can define rhetoric in purely negative terms as that which cannot be proven. All of this is rhetoric — everything that we can translate into language. For language belongs to it, and *logos* does too, because we can't translate anything into language without *logos.* You, on the other hand, are importing a compulsion into rhetoric that simply isn't there. If I forgive someone for something, I am not doing it because I think it will make me acceptable to him later on. No, that's not it; it isn't a purposive action.

D.: Isn't rhetoric goal-oriented?

G.: No, the concept of rhetoric is initially a very formal one, which is discourse of a kind that is not provable. It does belong to *eikos,* but it also belongs to thinking — thinking and speech. You, on the other hand, seem to see things as though rhetoric or discourse were only there to dissuade someone from the truth or to prove something untrue. On the contrary, in the case of rhetoric it's a question only of getting someone to understand our point of view or our opinion and communicating it to that person — just without being able to prove it. But to achieve this we need to put ourselves in the place of the other, and that means being genuinely considerate of the other without desiring to wage war on him. This is precisely what *syggnome* is — sympathetic insightfulness into the other. You have to keep a very broad conception of rhetoric in mind. And you can best do this if you think back to the second book of Aristotle's *Rhetoric*, where he talks about the emotions, about the passions.

D.: Yes, but that means that I must be aware of my passions in order to find the proper access to the other, that is, in order to be able to influence the other, or to influence others in a public gathering or the judge in a court of law. A theory of the passions is needed for that.

G.: Not just for that. For example, the first thing I really want when I love someone is to have the proper access to that person — that is *eros*. The *eros* problem is the other part of Platonic philosophy. Mathematics is not the most important thing in Plato, either. (I say "mathematics" for the sake of simplification; what I mean by this is science.) But I have to say, in all consciousness, that at our best we are in search of what is true. This must be the case because only then can we persuade the other of it. I am not trying to persuade someone of what I myself don't believe.

D.: But I can perhaps persuade the other of that which is useful to me.

G.: No, of that which I believe to be the case, that which I believe to be true. And when I am being of use to someone, then I'm certainly not doing that.

D.: No, of course not. But what I mean is that, according to Aristotle, rhetoric has three domains of application: first, the conversation or social interaction, then the *agora,* the plebiscite, and then the court of law. It's clear in all three cases that I always speak in my own interest and I always want to persuade the others of what is in my own interest.

G.: But this conception of rhetoric is very, very narrow, and this is why, for the Greeks, it's quite misleading if one begins with this conception alone. To the contrary, one must begin primarily from the idea that we have a great deal to say in life — and this is conversation, which is precisely the domain of rhetoric. The point of rhetoric is to teach one how to deliver or compose a speech so as to make possible a genuine understanding (*synesis*) and an authentic communication (*syggnome*), which constitute the basis for an actual consensus.

D.: But Aristotle himself also speaks of the *eikos,* the likely, as the basis of all rhetoric, and he teaches us precisely how we can work with it in speech in order to achieve a judgment or the consensus of the other. He offers the example of a small man who hits a larger one and is taken to court. His lawyer, of course, is supposed to say, "How could he have hit a man larger than himself?" This is the *eikos,* the likely; and he can presumably use it to persuade the judge that his client was in the right and is innocent of the charge.

G.: But only if the judge takes it to be true. The judge, however, is not a lawyer. The lawyer constructs the edifice of persuasion that the judge takes to be the truth.

D.: No, the lawyer *is* a rhetorician. For him, it's all about the result, and he wants to persuade the judge of a truth that is perhaps not the truth.

G.: But he considers it to be the truth. Inducing a judge to do something that he doesn't consider to be true doesn't really work.

D.: Yes, the judge is meant to consider it to be true, but it is quite different in the lawyer's case — and rhetoric is made for the lawyer.

G.: I don't know; perhaps it is made for the judge. The judge really shouldn't be taken in by rhetoric.

D.: I believe that the *Rhetoric* was written especially for lawyers and politicians who are striving precisely to reach consensus through their speeches.

G.: It was written for lawyers, for politicians, for everyone. And this is why he can refer to ethics in this context as well. He does this so he can base ethics on rhetoric as he introduces them both. Isn't this so?

D.: Yes, but ethics is something different from rhetoric.

G.: No, it *is* rhetoric — it is the rhetorical good. You need only to look it up in the text. What you say is incorrect. He has a much broader conception of rhetoric, one that coincides with the entire breadth of practical knowledge, that is, with *phronesis*. This is also why ethics belongs in there. And I see a development of rhetoric into ethics insofar as the concepts that constitute the foundations of rhetoric are worked out further in the *Ethics* — namely, genuine communication through speech, conversation, sympathetic insight into the other, consensus, and, finally, respect for the other, which stands higher than love, since all love is really a kind of will to power.

D.: But that was the objection that Derrida raised against you during that meeting in Paris that Phillipe Forget organized, was it not?[1] He thought that the power of good will that you spoke of was actually a good will to power.

G.: Well, yes, understanding good will in that way was quite an unfortunate misinterpretation of my German throughout the entire debate. He said that good will was really a will in the sense of the concept of will. That was not, however, what I meant. Rather, good will means not being prejudiced against others — this still means good will. This is why one says, "I want to listen with good will," hence *eumenes*, which is the Greek concept. We do use the expression "the will" for this, but it is not will in the sense of the will to power — it isn't that kind of will.

D.: Derrida's second objection to you was the question of your so-called *logocentrism*. By that he means any philosophical position that attributes everything to the *logos,* thus to reason, according to the Greek principle of *logon didonai,* "stating the reason" or "giving an account." In this basic attitude of Western thinking one sees in

---

1. Cf. Phillipe Forget, ed., *Text und Interpretation: Deutsch-Französische Debatte, mit Beiträgen von Jacques Derrida, Hans-Georg Gadamer, usw.* (Munich: Fink, 1984). [See also the English version of the debate and commentary in *Dialogue and Deconstruction: The Gadamer-Derrida Encounter,* ed. Diane P. Michelfelder and Richard E. Palmer (Albany, N.Y.: SUNY Press, 1989).]

logos the ultimate ground for the legitimization of every interpretation of the world. So, if interpreting means stating the reasons for
the interpretation, your hermeneutic philosophy (just like Heidegger's thinking and, of course, Hegel's as well) ultimately leads back
to the position that he simply calls "logocentrism." This phrase is
especially suited to Hegel, or, at least, it was coined specifically with
Hegel's thinking in mind. So he thinks that Nietzsche would have
been the only thinker to have escaped logocentrism, while Heidegger's
Nietzsche interpretation, which sees in Nietzsche a completion of
the modern metaphysics of subjectivity that is equivalent to Hegel's,
would itself succumb to logocentrism. On the other hand, deconstruction — Derrida's philosophy, that is — teaches us that every
interpretation of the world is nothing but a trace [*eine Spur*] that
we follow when we read a text. We have nothing but these traces,
which we follow to arrive at a possible destination.

G.: The second thing you said — or that he says — seems quite correct
to me or, at least, it seems to be the only thing that one can assert.
The other thing is precisely incorrect. In any case, I would say that
he most certainly did not mean Heidegger when he spoke of the will
to power in this sense.

D.: According to Heidegger, this would be the completion of metaphysics, the ultimate completion of metaphysics, where being is
understood as absolute will, just as in Hegel it was understood as
absolute knowledge.

G.: The error of metaphysics was that being was the dominant thing.
That was Heidegger's objection to Nietzsche. But there are other,
completely different kinds of will, for example (to stick with Aristotle and rhetoric), the kind that Aristotle himself speaks of in the
Rhetoric — namely, *orexis,* the purely emotional, which is the basic
mode of life itself. Nietzsche preferred to keep this kind of will in
mind — the authentic will to life, yes-saying to life, divorced from
any reason that we could furnish for it — we couldn't even *have* a
reason for it. Heidegger also says this — and this is not logic, and it's
not logocentrism either.

D.: Yes, certainly — it's just that the will, in Heidegger's sense, is a
metaphysical concept through which we are supposed to grasp reality
or a final principle. But now let's leave the matter of Nietzsche and

proceed to the same objection that Derrida also raises against hermeneutics — that hermeneutics is logocentrism. Are you concerned by this or not?

G.: First, I don't understand why hermeneutics would be logocentrism. I don't even understand what that would mean.

D.: It's simply that every interpretation is given on the basis of reasons, and it therefore also obeys the principle of reason, the principle of *logon didonai* or giving an account. Every interpretation, that is, claims to be correct and to be capable of providing reasons for its validity.

G.: No, I think that's patently untrue. For example, if I console someone who is in despair, then I am naturally seeking to make a "we" possible — that is, I am seeking to make possible that situation of mutual understanding and solidarity that is a dialogue. I neither have reasons to console him, nor can I simply say that I comfort him now so that I can do what I want with him later. This willing to console is not will to power, is it? I would dispute that absolutely. When good will is reduced to the will to the power, and when we think that we have to have reasons for everything, then we arrive, I freely admit, at the logic of Hegel, and this, of course, brings us to the will to power as the will to mastery — which is what Heidegger meant by technology. I would have no hesitation about saying this. If we can prove everything, if everything allows itself be proven, then we have indeed come very far. But along with what we can prove there is much that does not require proof. Here the role of the will is something different — it is only *orexis,* desire, appetite.

D.: And when it comes to interpretation? When, for example, we interpret one of Hegel's texts or a poem?

G.: Then it's entirely different. In that case, I listen very closely. With a poem or even a text... one must listen to the language, listen to what the poem or the text really wants to say. Obviously, every interpretation must go beyond what any logocentrism can recognize or claim to recognize. No, it was quite a gross misunderstanding of my position on the part of Derrida to interpret my will to understanding as a thoroughgoing Nietzscheanism, and, for the most part, the translation and the editing of the debate were at fault. Why Derrida was taken in by it, I don't know. But, in the meantime, Derrida and

I became quite well attuned to one another — after I made it clear in Naples that the horizon that one speaks of in the fusion of the horizons of interpretation is nothing that one ever reaches, so it can't assume a metaphysical position. Since then he has been entirely on my side. The horizon of interpretation changes constantly, just as our visual horizon also varies with every step that we take.

D.: Let's return now to the question of ethics and rhetoric. As I said, my impression is that you bring the two together too closely; they are, after all, two different fields of experience, and therefore we need two different disciplines or modes of investigation.

G.: There are surely differences as well. But, once again, these are classifications of the will on the part of mere thinking. I would venture to say that someone who is out to persuade doesn't think, "I am resolved to persuade someone. So, the next thing I will do is lie to him." That's not persuasion.

D.: No, Aristotle doesn't put it that way either. But he does say that we have to be able to help ourselves, and so we have to know how to make our own discourse robust and victorious by acknowledging the passions so as to make the most of them for our own purposes, or even by making whatever is more advantageous to us plausible.

G.: Yes, but the presupposition that one must make (and that one always denies) is always there — "Because I take it to be true." One desires to persuade just as the judge should also be persuaded — about what is true or about how something actually happened.

D.: I don't think Aristotle means it that way, because he says we find ourselves here, in the domain of the *eikos,* the likely, and not in the domain of the true itself.

G.: That just means "in dubio pro reo" — when we have no absolute certainty about the circumstances of an accusation, we should believe the accused. The judge thinks this way because he doesn't consider it to be proof (in sense that something cannot be proven that is not of the character of the mathematics), but he considers it, on the contrary, to be of the character of empirical knowledge. There is room here for mistakes, of course, and I don't say that misjudgments never occur. So, presumably, since no absolute certainty is possible, one must also believe. This is undoubtedly why this function belongs

to the judge as opposed to the lawyer — the judge doesn't want be lied
to. He wants to test the credibility of the assertion before the court.

D.: Fine. Now let's look at Sophism. It was surely true for Sophism —
for Protagoras, for Gorgias — that it isn't a matter of what is true or
false but only of persuading another of our point of view. We have
two opposing points of view before us with opposing reasons, and
someone can be taught how to lead either the one or the other to
victory. In the *Sophist,* Plato defines them precisely as teachers of
antilegein, the art of contradiction.

G.: That's Sophism — but rhetoric is something different. In the *Gorgias,* that is (in a positive sense, without drawing his conclusions from
Protagoras), he says quite explicitly that, no, rhetoric is none of that,
it's just the art of discourse. So only when this is denied does it become Sophism — that is, only when it is used simply as a means of
winning the fight. But only *if* it is used in this manner does it become
Sophism. As the art of discourse it is, instead, the power of *eros,*
which animates souls, or *phronesis,* reasonableness, which is meant
to bring us to consensus and to mutual understanding. *Phronesis* is
precisely not *deinotes* (which is mentioned explicitly in this passage),
cunning, or the possibility of those terrible men who can comprehend
everything immediately and can master and decide everything — this
is real will to power, and this is why those who have it are called
diabolical.

D.: I am gradually coming to understand the similarity between ethics
and rhetoric, even if I would still like to hold on to the difference.
So we are saying that in both cases it's a matter of mutual understanding, where there is precisely no truth in the sense of a provable
truth like there is in mathematics. But the difference between rhetoric
and ethics is that, through rhetoric (which has the three previously
mentioned applications in the domains of conversation, the *agora,*
and the court), we always want to persuade the other of our point of
view and proceed, so to speak, from our view of the matter, while,
in ethics, we have to proceed, above all, from our understanding of
the other.

G.: Certainly, but that is a very narrow conception of rhetoric, and
you have to understand it precisely. The *Gorgias* basically shows us
the struggle between the philosopher and the orator over the education of the youth. If it were it really like this — that on one side we

have the true and on the other side only deception or the subjection of things to one's own purpose — then it would never even come to such a struggle, not to mention a speech or a discussion where one defends one's point of view against another. It's quite clear that this is generally impossible because it would be wrong-headed to speak to someone who practically instantiates, so to speak, a form of will to power.

D.: But we are in the situation of having to defend ourselves. In a famous passage at the beginning of his *Rhetoric,* Aristotle himself says that the purpose of this study is to teach us how to defend ourselves with the word, since it would be unheard of to have to defend ourselves only with the body and not with *logos,* with speech.

G.: Yes, but we are to defend ourselves for the sake of *what?* For the sake of what is true! You simply put the rest behind it. Yet, what stands behind the whole of rhetoric is not power, as you presuppose, but coming to an understanding and the truth. Therein lies the distinction from the Sophist, who excludes the truth entirely, so to speak, and this is evidently why he brings to bear every possible argument with which to persuade the other. So rhetoric and Sophism *are* two different things, and yet this not to say that the other, the Sophist, doesn't apply rhetoric, for example, in developing an effective writing style. It's just that the Sophist alone makes use of it for his own advantage while the just speaker wants to arrive at the truth.

D.: So you don't differentiate rhetoric from ethics but from Sophism, and you shift the distinction between coming to an understanding and the sheer desire to persuade onto the distinction between Sophism and rhetoric. In this way, of course, you arrive at the conception of rhetoric that we had in Vico and his *Scienza Nuova.* But in rhetoric, then, is one's view also directed toward seeking the truth and wanting to persuade others of the truth?

G.: Yes. It might be, however, that one wants to lie to the other — but then we have Sophism.

D.: But should we come to the conclusion, then, that rhetoric doesn't merely have to do with the *eikos,* the likely, but that it has primarily to do with the true?

G.: Yes, of course. I think the point of the *Gorgias,* in fact, is that rhetoric is purely an instrument. This is entirely clear, and this is why rhetoric is dealt with extensively in the *Gorgias* — because with it one can distinguish between what is good and what is not good. I don't see what else there is to ask.

D.: Just this — that we began precisely from the idea that rhetoric has nothing to do with the true or with anything that one can prove. Now, to the contrary, we have come to the conclusion that rhetoric has the task of seeking and proving the truth, even though we are no longer in the domain of mathematics.

G.: Obviously, it has to do with what one takes to be true — I can't prove it, but I am persuaded that it is the case. As a judge, for example, I want to recognize the truth correctly, and this is why I think that truth and belief are distinct from one another. So it's really a question of distinguishing rhetoric from Sophism. When Gorgias, for example, seeks nothing but pure compassion, then this isn't Sophism. Sophism is something different — namely, when one can throw everything into a pot and do anything whatsoever just to win the argument. But this is precisely what the *Gorgias* does not do — even in its conclusions. Whenever you read the *Gorgias* dialogue like this and you try to draw this latter conclusion, then that's proto-Nietzschean or a prototype of Nietzsche — that's the will to power.

D.: Of course — but only because rhetoric has nothing to do with the truth.

G.: Yet it very well can if one is an honest man. Rhetoric doesn't necessarily make it false — it's just that one is delivered over into its power when one can prove everything or when one wants to prove everything. This is the extreme. Let's open Plato's *Gorgias* one more time to the point where we find the three levels of representation, along with their performers, Gorgias, Polus, Callicles. Here you have all the stages of genuine discourse, the claim to truth, and so on — there is still pure instrumentality in it across the board. This is why its value depends on its use.

D.: But this pure instrumentality teaches us to use Aristotelian rhetoric.

G.: But the real goal of the dialogue is to prove that the good speaker should use his art well, and when this art is used in a good way it induces those who make use of it to develop the proper sense of the just and the unjust. You must free yourself from this false conception of rhetoric as the art of appearances. Your conception of a merely instrumental rhetoric is incorrect. Vico stands squarely within the rhetorical tradition. He didn't invent anything. He was still holding on to something that became fixed in the overall development of antiquity, in the development of Greek and Roman culture. He simply reminds us once again that not everything is provable. In fact, he writes against Galileo and his conclusions. You have to get that through your head — and perhaps even more. We have become so confused by the last two hundred years that rhetoric has come to mean sheer rhetoric, nothing more — nothing but will to power. We need to see that, on the contrary, whenever anyone sets out to persuade, he himself also believes in what he is trying to persuade the other person of. Without this, then, rhetoric is empty rhetoric or, as we say, "hollow rhetoric."

5
Metaphysics and Transcendence

D.: Professor Gadamer, in our last conversation, the topic of which was rhetoric, we dealt with the question of whether rhetoric and ethics are the same discipline and whether both have the same domain of application. You were of the opinion that both were based on *phronesis* and, therefore, on the same domain of human discourse and communication. You further suggested that one cannot view rhetoric as a science in the strict sense, like mathematics. Though it does have to do with what is true, it belongs, not in the domain of the provable, but in the domain of human discourse. Now, what about metaphysics at its beginning in Aristotle? When a pupil of mine in Rome once posed to you the question of whether metaphysics were still possible, you answered that to do metaphysics we need two things: first a physics (and, at the time, this was Aristotelian physics) and then a mother tongue. So, does metaphysics, like rhetoric, also belong to the domain of human discourse, or does it, like physics, belong to the domain of science? I still remember that you often spoke of a book by Jakob Klein that provided you with some essential insights about this.

G.: I do indeed have my friend Jakob Klein and his book about Greek mathematics and logistics to thank for their clear insight into these problems. He wrote a truly classic essay on Greek mathematics[1] and thus bequeathed to me an insight into what *arche* really is for the Greeks — how it associates itself with the concept of number and how this concept develops itself further until eventually numeric or actual

---

1. See Jakob Klein, "Die griechische Logistik und die Entstehung der Algebra," in *Quellen und Studien zur Geschichte der Mathematik, Astronomie und Physik,* Edition B, Studies, vol. 3, Part 1 (1934): 18–105, Part 3 (1936): 122–235.

designations no longer stand for quantity and the one but are literary expressions instead. I realized that this was a very important moment for me — this was it! Abstraction had become so widespread by that time that a Galileo had become possible! It's really quite convincing! And one must also understand (and this also occurs in the book) that the first *arche*, the one, was *number*, and it only becomes *quantity* through its relation to the indeterminate duality. This book on Greek logistics and the emergence of algebra among the Greeks was a fundamental book for my understanding of the difference between the kind of knowing that for the Greeks is science and therefore belongs to pure *theoria* (the eternal and the perfectly observable) and, on the other hand, a different kind of knowing that falls into the domain of human communication. We should hold on to this distinction if we want to understand what physics and metaphysics were for Aristotle and what metaphysics in general can be or, at least, what we are doing when we associate ourselves with it. I also believe that, for Aristotle himself, physics and metaphysics and ethics are fundamentally different from science precisely because the Greeks viewed only strictly provable knowledge as science.

D.: For the Greeks, then, the exact science, that is, the objective and the groundable science, was mathematics. So one must differentiate it from knowledge that falls into the realm of human discourse and belongs in the domain of rhetoric. And, in your opinion, ethics also belongs to this domain?

G.: Of course. And this idea has been so covered over that people can't believe that ethics was once rhetoric. And what was physics, really? Aristotle never expressed himself on the topic. However, since it deals with motion it can be only a knowledge of the *epi to poly*, knowledge of that which happens for the most part. And such knowledge could only have been rhetoric. Generally speaking, the role that rhetoric undoubtedly played in physics was quite simply the same role that it played in every kind of knowledge that didn't possess the character of absolute provability — a characteristic belonging only to mathematics

D.: Are you sure that physics is dependent upon rhetoric as well?

G.: If Aristotle had to say what kind of science physics is (and he does say that there is *tyche* in it, chance) then it wouldn't be *episteme*

in the sense of the *Nicomachean Ethics*—most definitely not. What kind, then, would it be?

D.: Knowledge of reasons and *aitiai,* causes. The second book of the *Physics* speaks precisely of the four highest causes.

G.: Well, I would admit that, obviously. Nevertheless, I would have to say that these causes are clearly valid only in the domain of *peitho,* in the domain of that whereof there is persuasion and *epibole,* variation.

D.: Of course there is *epibole,* variation. But that changes nothing about the fact that the four causes constitute the structure, the framework of this *epi to poly.*

G.: If the causes (*aitiai*) were principles (*archai*) in the same the sense that the mathematical *archai* are, then you would be right. But the meaning of *aition* implies that there is sheer *epi to poly* and *tyche* in it, thus only the likelihood of what happens most of the time and by chance.

D.: But in the first book of the *Metaphysics,* Aristotle distinguishes *techne* or craftsmanship from *episteme,* science, precisely in that the former is only knowledge gained from the experience of what one is supposed to do, while *episteme,* on the other hand, is the knowledge of the *aitiai,* the grounds, the reasons for why something must be done. So, science is knowledge of the causes. In the *epi to poly* (what happens most of the time) there can thus be a concurrence of various causes, and whoever arrives at the correct causes and has a knowledge of them knows or has *episteme.*

G.: Then you no longer have chance. But that isn't Aristotle. In Aristotle, in the *Physics,* we do find chance and what happens most of the time. We therefore have to search for the *pythanon*—that which persuades us the most. This is why in the *Rhetoric, logos* is called a *dynamis*, a capacity, for seeing the *pythanon.*

D.: Perhaps in rhetoric; but in physics we are definitely not looking for that which persuades us the most—we are finding and indicating the causes.

G.: Yes, but everyone knows that this finding or knowing is very different from the knowledge of mathematics. The causes one seeks or finds are not actually the causes — or, rather, they *are,* but only as a rule. But what happens only as a rule in natural phenomena is what happens only most of the time and is exactly what recognizes the *epibole*. Physics is not an exact science; it is just an empiricism.

D.: I would say, to the contrary, that the *Physics* tries to teach us how to construct a science from an empiricism.

G.: I don't think Aristotle argued in that way.

D.: Why, then, at the beginning of the *Metaphysics,* does he distinguish these three steps: *empeiria* (empiricism), *techne* (craftsmanship or technique), and *episteme* (science)?

G.: Because he wants to clarify the place of knowledge. There can indeed be various kinds of knowledge, yet not every knowledge is certain knowledge.

D.: Yes, exactly. If there is an *epi to poly,* there are also various ways in which one knows about it. There is, to be precise, *empeiria* — knowledge of that which is usually the case — by means of which doctors (who at that time were called *empeirioi*) could practice their profession. There is a *techne* or a knowledge not just of that which is the case as a rule, but of how to make something so that the thing keeps functioning like one wants it to. And there is the third level that consists of the people who know why the thing is thus and why it functions thus, while the others know only that it is *epi to poly* — only that it is so most of the time. This third kind of knowledge is a knowledge of the *aitiai,* the causes. They can indicate the reason why it happens thus, and this constitutes *episteme.*

G.: It doesn't constitute the conception of *episteme* that we find in the *Nicomachean Ethics.* The concept of science that we have in the *Ethics* refers only to things that do not change. Physics, therefore, cannot be a science in this sense.

D.: Well, then, let's say that what is presented at the beginning of the *Metaphysics* pertains to a different science, precisely the science of final reasons and causes, which serves the purpose of substantiating what is acknowledged in physics, and this means that it leads back to a genuine *episteme* that is no longer physics but precisely metaphysics.

G.: Does the name John Cleary mean anything to you? He is a pupil of mine who just wrote a good book on the Greeks and mathematics.

D.: Yes, I know him. Doesn't he propose the thesis in his book that the Greeks didn't apply mathematics to physics, or that they weren't yet familiar with the concept of a mathematized physics that arises with Galileo and Newton?

G.: No, he didn't try to deny that. He just said that it wasn't yet generally the case at the time. It was certainly true that there was something generally like mathematics. It first became something particular among the Greeks. It begins very early and develops gradually. . . .

D.: But if we now go back to the point of our discussion, the bone of contention was that in physics one can never arrive at the *episteme* that is there in the *Ethics* and in mathematics. Now, I know Cleary very well, and he once explained to me that the Greeks didn't have this Galilean conception of the kind of mathematics that makes knowledge in physics possible for us — as exact and universal knowledge, that is.

G.: Yes, precisely.

D.: Fine, those were two different domains. But I mean something quite different, which is that the knowledge of physics makes metaphysics as a true knowledge possible for us by means of the science of first principles and causes.

G.: In truth . . . physics was already a dilemma, and metaphysics is still one — so, we have a double dilemma.

D.: Metaphysics is conceived precisely for the sake of grounding physics and resolving these dilemmas. Metaphysics is precisely the *prote episteme, the* science, or the science of beings as beings. It turns the first principles of beings into the objects of investigation, and this is precisely how it can ground physics. Even you have always said that the *Metaphysics* shouldn't have ended with Book *Lambda,* with the science of *aidion,* eternal being or the divine — it should have just remained the science of first principles and causes or the science of being, as such. But that would mean that it should have remained a foundation for the *Physics — meta ta physika.*

G.: I understand. Nevertheless, I still have certain difficulties, because for me, oddly enough, Book *Lambda* of the *Metaphysics,* to this day, contains a mysterious leap. First the role of the relative is laid out, then the related concepts, and then, all of a sudden, comes the thesis. Werner Jaeger, in his time, didn't consider this book to be a unified lecture that stood by itself, and this wasn't entirely unwarranted. Nor can one deny that, as the matter stands now, it creates the impression of a leap at this point. It doesn't make sense to say the one thing first and then the other. So, the great riddle for me is always how theology, all by itself, becomes metaphysics, which, strictly speaking, had not yet occurred to Speusippus (Plato's first student), who was the one who worked it out. So, to that extent, I am always having difficulties. I admit it. I don't say you're wrong. I only ask, what does *episteme* (science) really mean? *Episteme* is surely something more than bare logic. In the *Metaphysics* logic is what you can demonstrate — something whereby the *aitia,* the cause, becomes understandable. This is what happens here. Generally speaking, this is the case. I can't imagine that the whole problem of Tübingen Platonism would exist if you were correct. In fact, I find what they do quite crazy. But the reason I find it crazy is that they naively translate the essence of mathematics, as it were, into philosophy, and I think this is incorrect. There is no debate about this in the whole of Hellenism. At best, you can find it among the Sceptics, but I don't know enough about it there. So I'm still a little hesitant. We could concede at this point that there is a broader concept of *episteme* and a narrower one. The narrower concept is doubtless that of mathematics. All knowledge must be derived from certainty, from the truth. In Aristotle, this is not the case for any natural law. What else should *epi to poly* and *tyche* mean if not this, which is certainly quite reasonable, but . . . there are exceptions.

D.: I think we must now take into account those two basic Aristotelian concepts, *dynamis* and *energeia,* which (as Heidegger reminds us) were very badly translated in our Latin tradition by *potentia* and *actus,* possibility and actuality. So we should say that there is *dynamis,* and through this there are *epi ta poly* and *tyche,* chance. So it isn't true, as Tugendhat thinks (I heard this from him in a Heidelberg seminar), that *dynamis* and *energeia* are the same thing. Through *dynamis* there is chance, and, on the other hand, through *energeia* there is an *eidos,* an appearance, that presupposes *dynamis* but is, nevertheless, an *eidos,* a stable form.

G.: An interesting question, but I have to think about it. At first glance, it's not all that clear to me. But obviously I can understand how one could loosen up one's conception of *episteme.*

D.: That's precisely what Aristotle is trying to do — he's trying to break loose from Platonism while, nevertheless, still adhering to it in order to ground an *episteme*; and this is what the idea of *dynamis-energeia* means. There is also an *entelecheia* (a working toward an end), which has even found a place in Kant, if only in the form of a subjective maxim of our power of judgment. There can be exceptions, and nevertheless we cannot doubt that this principle of the end helps us to extend our knowledge of nature. This isn't Platonism but it is a metaphysics, that is, a possible grounding for an *episteme* that discloses a structure of being qua being by which physics can then be supported.

G.: I do understand that, but I would still have to think about it. Frankly, it makes me uneasy because Plato has yet to be connected with Aristotle, even though I have constantly tried to demonstrate this connection.

D.: On this point, we would like to ask you whether your clarification of Plato's and Aristotle's thinking doesn't offer us new possibilities for taking up the metaphysical problematic once again — on a dialogical basis. Is there just the one possibility that the Tübingen school and its Italian followers have offered us, or are there also possibilities besides the one you just mentioned?

G.: It's more a question of my saying that these are two entirely different things. On the one hand, the question that you pose is proper: What do I understand by metaphysics? Is it the case that all of metaphysics has come an end, or what else could be the case? One answer to this is completely different from the one that follows if you accept the Tübingen Plato interpretation, which we have spoken of already. I can bring the two together, but only because you're doing it. With all due respect, I don't find what the Tübingen school does at all important — particularly in relation to metaphysics. It's poorly done. It's as if Aristotle's colleague who endorsed the last of the research that he did and from which the ultimate truth was to be expected were Aristotle himself. Yet it would be idiotic to use these few lines that someone dug up out of a cellar a century before Christ as an argument for metaphysical truth. As I see it, the Tübingen school teaches us that we must ultimately begin to read Aristotle in this manner as well — that is, to read the notes of Aristotle as obviously notes for a lecture course and not as a book. This is what Jaeger argued, and that was fine, even though, on the whole, his point was exaggerated and so it ultimately foundered. The *Ethics,* whatever else it was, was something Jaeger couldn't account for. Well, in any case, this is as far as we have come today. And this is why I'm not all that interested in the Tübingen school — they are now actually taking up Proclus again, which is why everything is distorted to begin with. This is bad enough, of course, but there are two things to be discussed here. One is, in fact, what you call "metaphysical thinking," because we can only be rationally complete with a concept of transcendence. And I would say that we certainly must be aware of this — this is the task of philosophy today. Having said that, I am also of the opinion that philosophy is preparing the ground for a global conversation, and we must take advantage of this opportunity and develop a dialogue, or we will be lost.

D.: A world-historical conversation among the religions, or what?

G.: A conversation among the religions. Certainly, because the great world religions do exist. But, then... not really "among" the religions. I think you understood me correctly. I would just express it more carefully. Let's ask, rather, "How is the Enlightenment comprehended among these religions?" Even now, you see, even now it is clear to me that the same thing by no means follows from the world-view of Japan, for example, as it does for us. It's really like this — in the great chain of the experience of transcendence, only one experience has been salvaged in our case, and that, to be precise, is Calvinism.

D.: "In our case" — by this you mean Northern Europe, and one should perhaps also include North America, where an open possibility still exists. Whereas, in your opinion, Japan has already "crossed the line" of nihilism, to use one of Ernst Jünger's expressions?

G.: Certainly. Nothing definite comes from Japan — nothing to speak of; and from China — once again, nothing. At the moment, of course, China is communistic or who knows what — perhaps a full-blown communism....

D.: But is that the equivalent of a full-blown capitalism?

G.: Yes, exactly. I want to say again that, on the whole, one must frame the question from the very beginning by pointing out that we should not understand this conversation as a conversation between the representatives of religions or between philosophers — for example, between Wittgenstein and me or between Wittgenstein and Heidegger. These accomplish nothing; they are infinitesimally small accommodations. I could very quickly force myself to conform to the late Wittgenstein, but I mustn't do that. I could very easily say, "You see, I am really in complete agreement with the late Wittgenstein, and I call that hermeneutics!"

D.: Do you think — as has often been said — that the concept of the language game can easily be seen as coinciding with the concept of the hermeneutic circle? This is presumably why you were able to accept the concept of the language game.

G.: Yes, the concept of the language game and also the concept of individuality. Anything else won't work. The concept of an ideal language proved untenable for him. This is why the first answer that I have to give about the dialogical possibility of metaphysical discourse is this dialogue between the various world religions, which philosophy should prepare because it discovers within everyone an instance of the great chain that we call transcendence. The problem is whether this dialogue of the religions themselves is possible and whether one can actually arrive at it by going beyond the philosophical discussion. I say this because I am convinced that we are in a hopeless situation, and that it is, in fact, the necessary consequence of the one-sidedness of a purely scientific knowing. We can make good use of the natural sciences, but the idea that we can now solve all our problems, like birth and death, history and purpose of life, with this conception of truth — that makes no sense. It's neither here nor there. . . . Nothing, of course, can come of it.

But neither can we simply shove these problems to the side. And if I were to respond right now to the Tübingen school, then first thing I would say is, "How are we ourselves suppose to know anything?" For that matter, how is it that I myself think anything at all? As usual, the obvious answer would be "the will of God." But, perhaps we can say something even better — even to some extent about Neo-Platonism. We cannot, for example, hide the fact that we can't simply revoke Neo-Platonism. So, for us, transcendence is a very good expression to use for saying that we aren't certain what there is in the beyond or what it is like. None of us can say that we have any mastery over the beyond. We simply can't say anything about a lot of things — about the mysteries of birth, life, and death. We will probably tackle the two first problems soon. Perhaps birth will no longer be a mystery, but rather something that will come completely within the grasp of bioengineering — we do, after all, have an egg to work with. But, presumably, science cannot reach the ultimate in this case either. Probably not everything will become artificial for us, because that's something that humbles us as human beings. Birth and motherhood are truly in the nature of the human female, and the distinction between this and the artificial would really become noticeable. This is why I doubt that it would ever be accepted in exactly the same way.

The result of these considerations is, first of all, that I think Wittgenstein is unjustly interpreted as being nihilistic. I also don't believe that everything for him is just language games — this is not the decisive thing. The decisive thing is that Wittgenstein generally omits any opinions about such things as death or life. I think he does leave room for such problems, and it's certain that he never quite got entirely free of his Catholic boyhood.

D.: So Wittgenstein wasn't a nihilist. Now, what do you think of Karl Popper and his Plato interpretation?

G.: In Popper's case, it's simply ludicrous that he should always deny the beyond. And one has to take a stand with respect to his Plato interpretation, and I did this, albeit not with a lot of success, especially not in America. I find it quite splendid that there's never unanimity in science, not even with its concepts, so that a variety of opinions still predominates. When Popper was a young man, he was a good theoretician of logic and argumentation, and I was quite satisfied with him, but later this was no longer possible for me. I think that if one concedes the proposition that it's necessary to occupy oneself with transcendence, then one can no longer travel the path of Popper. This has nothing to do with him personally, but one can no longer speak to him on these terms.

D.: Now that we have discussed your place in contemporary thinking and heard your judgments on the great thinkers of today, we can turn to the great philosophies of the previous century and concentrate, first, on the one thinker who is as present in your philosophy as Plato and Aristotle — I mean Hegel.

G.: Ah, Hegel. I have to say with all sincerity that I have always had a great admiration for him, and I still do today. But he isn't on the right path at the moment, but rather Schelling is, which is something Heidegger always understood as well. Do you remember the statement he made in a seminar he held in Marburg, "Show me a single proposition in Hegel's philosophy that has the depth of Schelling's assertion that 'Anxiety before the nothing drives creatures out from their center' "?

D.: Yes, you quoted this expression of Heidegger's and the statement from Schelling quite often. It's from Schelling's treatise *On the Essence of Human Freedom,* isn't it?

G.: Yes, precisely. In any case, I would say at the outset that the difference between Hegelian philosophy (which interprets itself in a Protestant way) and Schelling's appears to consist in the fact that Schelling — in spite of his philosophical interpretation of Christianity — ultimately remains a Christian. Hegel, on the other hand (even though he does not, of course, subsume [*aufhebt*] Christianity — he, too, remains a Christian, a Protestant Christian), through sheer self-reflection ultimately no longer takes revelation seriously (much like Bultmann).

D.: Do you think that in Hegel's case we have an emptying of the real content of Christian revelation or, rather, a philosophical interpretation that subsumes [*aufhebt*] it within his comprehensive thinking according to the triple meaning of the concept *aufheben,* which means *tollere* as well as *conservare* and *elevare*? He thought he could take up [*aufheben*] the content of revelation (which we refer to as transcendence) into the movement of thought, that is, bring it along with it in order to explain it, interpret it, and so on. . . .

G.: But look, this transcendence is really a more fundamental one. There's no such thing any more as a metaphysics that believes it has a truth that withstands everything — none of us has this kind of truth. We have to say that none of us knows anything, but we have learned to believe otherwise. And this is no doubt because at one time or another we all make an attempt to become acquainted, so to speak, with the wonders of life and death — just as we do with our own lives. This is simply how it is. What, then, is philosophy? A knowing that is quite restricted and circumscribed by limits. This, then, is why we have hermeneutics — why we have a transcending of these limits. It's the same for Heidegger — we never know what being is. It always seems to be a *topos,* an unattainable place that never becomes accessible. That's how it works in *Being and Time*: I never know anything about being — perhaps I do know something about it as *Ereignis,* but perhaps not, because every *Ereignis* is basically ungraspable, indeterminable. . . .

D.: As far as that goes, do you think that the so-called "turn" is a return, a turning back toward the origin or toward the originary moment of *Being and Time*?

G.: Of course — a return to being, which is really thought as transcendence, and so it appears as *Ereignis*. For this is nothing but being presenting itself to us and appearing, relative to us, through time, since time already constitutes the horizon of the question of being and even appears as the meaning of being itself. Being's relation to us through time, *Ereignis,* remains incomprehensible because being is precisely transcendence.

D.: Here, again, I have to pose a question to you. Heidegger himself, in *Kant and the Problem of Metaphysics,* equates finitude and transcendence, for he thinks that we are finite precisely insofar as we are compelled to transcend the field of experience. This idea is exactly the basis of Kant's conception of the transcendentals or the transcendentality of recognition. Because of its finitude, our understanding must adhere to these reference points in the field of experience as conditions for the possibility of knowledge, and that would be the initial transcendence of our sensory experience. Now, since we were talking about Hegel, couldn't we say (along with Hegel, particularly in his *Science of Logic*) that we have a thoroughgoing transcendentality that also includes history, religion, and art and brings them to a complete interpretation?

G.: Here is where I would be a little more cautious. In fact, this is why I insist so much on Schelling, who arrived at the concept of "the immemorial."[2] I think this is true for Hegel as well. Yet in his private life he clearly remained a Protestant Christian, and he evidently assumed this in his theories without speaking of it openly as such.

D.: Of course. Could we say, then, that his position is a thoroughgoing Protestantism in the sense of a complete interpretation of the

---

2. [Literally, "the un-pre-thinkable," *das Unvordenkliche* is sometimes translated slightly more literally, albeit somewhat more awkwardly, as "the unpremeditatable."]

Christian doctrine of salvation, but one that refuses to acknowledge any mediator, any external authority, or any church — a complete interpretation that orients itself only to the *logos* or allows itself to be guided only by the *logos,* by thinking? Or is there also a place in his thinking for a transcendence that is not *logos*? We have seen that there is such a place in Schelling. But is there in Hegel as well?

G.: In Hegel's case, well . . . I believe Hegel would have demurred here as well. He wouldn't have answered the question, that is, he would have stayed away from it.

D.: But in Hegel we have absolute knowing at the end of the *Phenomenology of Spirit* — that is to say, at the end of the long path of the development of consciousness in its historical experience.

G.: This is certainly implied at the end of his *Philosophy of Spirit,* but even the *Logic* repeatedly assumes the improvement of the human being to be possible. He considers the human being to be capable of improvement. In the *Logic,* this is the basic comportment of the human being that he refers to as absolute knowing. After all, absolute knowing occurs right alongside art and religion, which are also absolute — that is, they occur *along with it* as the absolute. One is not subsequent to the other. This relationship is certainly different than it is in Schelling, but it's not entirely different — it isn't the idea that we have to reduce everything to science.

D.: So is absolute knowing the knowledge of the absolute on the part of finite spirit, which is conscious of its finitude as well as its absolute possibility for improvement?

G.: Yes, and that leads us again to the special kind of knowing that is *phronesis,* wisdom. Here we should formulate a basic principle or, if you will, a first proposition — *phronesis* is evidently the most important of all the developments of practical philosophy, of ethics; and one must further acknowledge that this was all there was in ethics at the outset of Greek history. First, there was Pyrrhonism, then Scepticism, then came Platonism. But in the end the same thing comes back again. So, once again, this means that what we must also keep in mind here is that transcendence is not attainable anywhere. Transcendence is not simply believing in God. It is something incomprehensible, and this is true for Hegel as well. This is all we can say today. It's also true for

Jaspers, who incorporated this form of transcendence into his thinking, but even for Heidegger. This is why we ourselves (and Heidegger as well) have, for some time, been able to come to an extensive understanding with Jaspers. I have to say that these are all of the things that I appreciate about Jaspers — they occur in his three volumes of philosophy, particularly the beautiful little work on Kierkegaard and the one on *Nietzsche and Christianity* — not, however, the Nietzsche book; that one's not important. So I would basically agree with Jaspers that the *ignoramus* is the fundament of transcendence.

D.: The *ignoramus* (ignorance), then, is finitude?

G.: Yes, it's the finitude beyond which we are not allowed to go. I think, then, that we really have to conclude from this that it's wrong to hope for something from any of the possible forms of nihilism, be it Stalinism or Leninism, which is perhaps a little better. None of it has worked well. We must admit to ourselves that humanity is searching — looking everywhere — for something different. The most divers religions constitute the most divers responses to this search. This is why we must also learn to live together in this way with those who are different.

D.: And also come to a mutual understanding among ourselves?

G.: By "in this way," I mean "with respect." We must learn to come to an understanding with and to respect ourselves. I don't think I can solve the problems that result from the question of human rights either. For instance, if the Chinese who want to settle here never properly adapt themselves to our state system, then we must remember that they never had a constitutional state in our sense — we have to take that into account. I don't think, however, that this constitutes an objection to the idea that we have to try to come to an understanding.

D.: So, since we're now talking as philosophers about the path of our future and about what awaits us, what, then, do you think of the "last god" that Heidegger speaks of in the *Spiegel* interview and his assertion that only it could save us? What do you think he meant by this?

G.: I don't want to express myself on that just yet. I don't know anything other than the fact that, at the outset, anyone in history or society who is "a dominant one" or one who is "for something" or "against something" is simply imagined away — there is surely no doubt about this. So, we know nothing about how the beyond could fulfill itself here or how the *ignoramus* is to be overcome instead of increasing itself. For that matter, I think, as far as he was concerned, he was being consistent in his adherence to the doctrine of the Catholic Church rather than inconsistent. We are exposed to the beyond in our self-awareness. Whether or not there is life after death or some such thing, he would neither have wanted to accept it nor to deny it any more than I would. The really good Catholics said nothing about it. Guardini was once asked by someone about this, and he said he believed in a reunion with our dead loved ones — his wife, for instance. This is how he saw it, which is fine because none of the really dogmatic things existed for him — just this reunion.

D.: So, is it just a matter here of interpreting this doctrine, or will one arrive at the true Gospel in the interpretation? For Bultmann (as for the entire Protestant Evangelical Church, for that matter), there still is a revelation and a life after death.

G.: Bultmann is actually supposed to have spoken about this at length in the memorial speech for Guardini. When it comes to revelation, the problem is whether he didn't completely distort it with his interpretation.

D.: Do you mean his interpretation of the Prologue to the Gospel of John which, for Bultmann, is supposed to be a Neo-Platonic hymn?

G.: No, it wasn't just the Prologue, it was the entire Gospel of John that he read in terms of Neo-Platonism. I think he later abandoned this, but it wasn't quite clear to me whether it actually dealt with a process of the movement of reflection and not something else. I couldn't say, therefore, whether Bultmann might not have ended up in the same position as Hegel, which is, of course, different from Schelling's position. In Bultmann, of course, in place of Hegel's absolute knowing we have the faith of human existence in the Gospel. But the problem is whether absolute knowing is not itself a principle for interpreting the content of revealed religion — the Christian religion — which, according to Hegel, it expressed in the form of the Idea. But this is nothing other than what the philosophy of existence calls "faith" or, at least, faith in a determinate content of revelation, which it also wants to interpret.

6
Ethics and Politics

D.: Professor Gadamer, today we would very much like to pose the question of the relationship between philosophy and politics and to work through it with you thoroughly. This became a burning question at the end of the 1960s with the student movement, and your confrontation with Habermas, which he published in his Suhrkamp volume *Hermeneutik und Ideologiekritik,* dates back exactly to this period. The question of the critique of ideology was more or less the question of a critique of the existing political circumstances and of legitimate authority in general. This is precisely why, before we come to the problem of politics, I would very much like to ask you how your relationship with Habermas began, which, after all, lasted for a long time and played an important role for both of you.

G.: Habermas was really a personal discovery of mine. It happened essentially out of the desire for the review[1] to get a detailed account of Marxism and of the whole literature of Marxism. The literature is quite voluminous, and his account was composed in two parts. It wasn't overly verbose — on the contrary, it was very, very well done. And it impressed me very much that he bracketed out the political commentary altogether and pursued only the logical, the, so to speak, technically demonstrable argumentation.

D.: You're referring to his work *The Logic of the Social Sciences,* which originally appeared as a special edition of the *Philosophische Rundschau*?

G.: Yes, that's the work. It was my initiative, and I was convinced that he was just what we needed. In the beginning, however, I had a difficult confrontation with Löwith, because at first it was very hard for me to get him to accept Habermas. Löwith really wanted

1. [*Philosophische Rundschau*]

to have Apel, but I said, "No, I'd prefer to have someone who does something that we can't do." Apel was already well known. He was a very serious man — even a Rothacker student, just like Habermas — and it was a very close call. But I defended myself this time and stood firm for Habermas. Something else came into it — the fact that at one time it was a feature of earlier academic life that one didn't need to have done a habilitation thesis. Heisenberg, for example, had been such a case.

D.: Heisenberg, the famous physicist, had only written a doctoral dissertation and not a habilitation thesis?

G.: No, not the physicist but his father. The father, that is, was a teacher at a school for Eastern studies and was called to Munich without a habilitation thesis. And so, through my father and through my acquaintances, I was already thoroughly familiar with idea of someone being appointed directly without having habilitated. That was how things worked at that time with good teachers. So I fought for him — I really wanted to push this through. Löwith finally relented and said, "If you want it this way, maybe it will be all right after all. I have no further objections." But for me the real point was to get the faculty to allow Habermas to examine people, assign doctoral theses, confer degrees, and so on.[2] So I said, "Do you trust me? If you trust me, allow this venerable old custom to stand." I was later informed that Horkheimer and Adorno had had a falling out over Habermas. Adorno was probably too far to the left. Horkheimer, at any rate, was a good teacher — unlike Adorno.

D.: Was it, perhaps, that he talked too much?

G.: Yes, but he wrote very well in those days, in contrast to his lectures. Horkheimer's lectures, on the other hand, were excellent — exceptionally good. In any case, they quarreled for political reasons. Horkheimer hadn't wanted to accept Habermas' habilitation thesis — his essay on the public sphere.[3] The book isn't really all that philosophical. Nevertheless, I found it to be rather good after I got to know his other book, *The Logic of the Social Sciences.* So I managed to

---

2. Habermas confirmed all of this to us word for word.

3. This refers to the essay that later became his famous book, *Strukturwandel der Öffentlichkeit,* 2d ed. (Frankfurt am Main: Suhrkamp, 1962, 1990). [English edition: *The Structural Transformation of the Public Sphere,* trans. Thomas Burger, with Frederick Lawrence (Cambridge, Mass.: MIT Press, 1992).]

convince myself that his philosophy wasn't really monotonous. I also discovered that it must not have been Löwith who didn't agree with me — it had to have been Habermas who disagreed with me, quite explicitly — and that proved to be colossal. Unfortunately, he stayed in Heidelberg only three and a half years — from 1958 to 1962, I believe. It wasn't a matter of his contradicting me — on the contrary, what I strove for, above all, was that the people who come to work with me should be the same people who work with others who represent the opposite position. That wasn't entirely the case with Löwith. Anyone who went to work with him after having latched himself firmly to me found Löwith boring. Conversely, the people who were normally accustomed to Löwith found me unintelligible — Koselleck, for example, who was primarily with Löwith.

D.: Then did Habermas do his degree and habilitate with Löwith?

G.: No, no. He did his degree with me. Then he did his habilitation thesis with the historians.

D.: What fascinated you at the time about Habermas — other than the fact that he knew Marxism so well, which, of course, was a fashionable philosophy at the time?

G.: I was fascinated by his ability to have a political opinion and, when invited by a philosophical journal to write about the corresponding philosophical literature, not to engage in political propaganda but, instead, to lay out the various weaknesses in the theories. I looked at the work again recently, and, once again, I found that he had done it quite properly. One also sees how educable he was. Since then, however, he has frequently been taken in by things. Things, however, were not entirely peaceful in the beginning. He attacked me on the question of authority — although he lost that battle very quickly. For I only had to say to him, "What do you mean? All I have ever said is that one cannot appeal to authority. One *has* authority, but one can never *appeal* to it — that's just how it works." He understood it then — it also worked this way with psychoanalysis.

D.: Speaking of psychoanalysis, Habermas thought, at the time, that it could free us from the unconscious forms of authority that operate in our unconscious minds and inhibit us and keep us in thrall. In this sense, psychoanalysis would have the same emancipatory power as the critique of ideology and also perform the same function.

G.: Yes, exactly, and I talked him out of this idea as well. "Talked him out of" is not perhaps the right expression. I don't believe he gave the two ideas up for my sake; he was just more discerning — he was educable. I wouldn't, however, say that *I* learned very much from *him,* because he then left immediately for Konstanz. If he had been there longer, I would perhaps have learned something from him, for that's how it happens with students — even if it happens indirectly. It was a bit more like that with Koselleck, from whom I did learn because he was there longer.

D.: But there was also a third theme to the discussion. Number one was the critique of authority — he thought philosophical re-flection should be a critique of authority. The second theme was psychoanalysis, which teaches us how one can dismantle unconscious authority or social compulsion. The third point was the anticipation of true life. Habermas declares that emancipatory reflection, which is the heritage of German Idealism, teaches us to dissolve our inher-ent nature through the anticipation of true life. You thought (I don't know whether you remember it) that this was romanticism, while Habermas was firmly convinced that the romanticism was on your part in that you stuck precisely to the conservative side of romanti-cism through your conception of authority and tradition or, at least, the authority and values of the tradition.

G.: Yes, yes, I remember it well enough. But, after having occupied himself with topics in the philosophy of right and getting involved in the American discussion of civil rights, he no longer thinks that way, and he no longer speaks that way either. He realized, of course, how much the legitimation of legal norms is grounded in the strength of one's own legal tradition.

D.: So did he realize the value of the tradition for legitimating the genuine authority of legal norms?

G.: Yes, I think he has now gotten beyond this question of the cri-tique of the authority carried by the historical strength of the cultural tradition. He no longer talks that way, and he no longer criticizes me from this perspective.

D.: As I understand it, Apel is now annoyed with him because he no longer criticizes Gadamer. Earlier on, however, Habermas had insisted on this criticism against you, and he always thought that authority could be legitimized only through critique, particularly through the critique of ideology, which is precisely what should have taken the place of hermeneutics. In his opinion, when it comes to political conservativism and the sheer authority of tradition, hermeneutics comes to a halt.

G.: I know, I know. It all began at a meeting in Mannheim at which he and Hans Albert were present along with some of my students (Volkmann-Schluck among others), and these two ascribed a completely misplaced concept of authority to me. It had nothing to do with what I meant by authority, and this is why I reacted against it so vehemently, and, for my part, I objected to their assertions by asking, "What do you have against authority? How can you understand authority in this completely external sense, as if authority were just external compulsion?" But now, after all of the experiences he has had, I think he has freed himself from this conception of authority. Authority is certainly not external compulsion, but rather that which has thoroughly permeated common customs, common practices, legislation, revolutions, and so forth and managed to resist the destructive force of criticism in such a way that it has ultimately been accepted by all the members of a society. I was only trying to point out how authority has established itself gradually throughout history, and I was trying to say that you shouldn't pretend to know how authority arose in the course of history — you couldn't know this. Only when you realize that you have actually achieved a certain authority will you perhaps know something about it.

D.: This was also the sense of the objections that they raised against him in America and from which he essentially learned something, isn't it? Laws, practices, and customs legitimize themselves and, consequently, their authority as well?

G.: Of course. For that matter, the principle I so often cite also applies here: "Whoever appeals to authority has no authority." Authority legitimizes itself in precisely the same way that customs, practices, and the laws arising from them do. But all such critiques and polemics had arisen solely from the intensification of the political struggle. This struggle, meanwhile, is now in the past — it's all in the past.

D.: How, then, do you see the further development of his own thinking, that is, his theory of communicative action, which introduces a new phase of his philosophy that we could also refer to as his post-Marxist phase? Do you think the concept of communicative action is a further development of his concept of communicative competence, which he had already spoken of at the time of the debate about *Hermeneutics and the Critique of Ideology,* and which you criticized?

G.: Yes. In fact, it seems to me that his thinking actually comes to an end with the concept of communicative competence, which I did criticize at the time. I criticized it because it was coupled with the acquisition of behavioral roles in society — as if there were a linguistic-communicative competence that one acquires in precisely the same way that one acquires a social role. This is why I was against the concept of communicative competence.

D.: But isn't this concept derived from Chomsky's concept of linguistic competence? Chomsky, that is, distinguishes between the *competence* and the *performance* of the speech act, thereby distinguishing linguistic competence, which is acquired with the mother tongue, from linguistic action.

G.: Perhaps one can speak of language competence in this way, as Chomsky does, even though this expression doesn't suit me; but it means nothing more than the acquisition of one's own mother tongue. On the other hand, if one were to take it seriously, communicative competence would mean nothing more than the ability to have a conversation. But this is just a personal ability and even a personal task. If, on the other hand, it's coupled with the acquisition of a social behavioral role, then it becomes a technology and a determinate social factor within a society. But then we are no longer dealing with genuine personal communication, which is just as free and personal as the use of our mother tongue. On the other hand, it becomes the object of a sociology, that is, a scientific examination of the social factors of behavioral roles, which its knowledge puts at the disposal of the social engineer but which, as I have already said, "only produces, without setting free" [*nur herstellt, ohne freizustellen*].

D.: Does this critique run parallel to the critique of his examination of psychoanalysis as a model for the critique of ideology? Would it free us from the disruptive factors of our behavior that are to be attributed to inner compulsions, just as the critique of ideology frees us from external compulsions?

G.: Of course. The same principle applies here. The analyst is in his proper place as a doctor whenever he accepts the needy patient into his practice in order to help him. But if he were to go outside of his practice and, in the course of normal social interaction, question his cohorts like patients about the unconscious factors of their behavior in order to free them from possible ideological disorders, then he would fall out of his role of social partner and become a know-it-all whom people would avoid. He would also fall back into the role of the social engineer who desires to produce without setting free.

D.: So do you think that Habermas, with his theory of communicative action, still somehow persists in an uncritical conception of science that allows him to remain rooted in a sociology of knowledge and makes it impossible for him to engage in philosophy properly?

G.: The point, it seems to me, is that in Heidelberg he had a genuine conception of critical theory that didn't really stem from Marxism. It came, instead, as he himself recognized, from the critical power of the reflection of German Idealism. This is why I believed, and I still say this today, that the real question is, "What did he do after he went away?" He occupied himself with social science — that is to say, he was doing the one thing that is of the least importance to me, namely, reaching out to the citizenry and not to the human being as such. He did what the Marburg school had always done as well, which is to say, "Look how right I am." They appealed only to idiots and young people. As I understood it, the assertion that Neo-Kantianism always made was, "Science shows us things." And this stuck with Habermas — although what he meant was, "Science brings us insight."

D.: Science, in other words, brings us insight into the true life or the anticipation of the true life.

G.: And that's why I was against it — not so much against the true life, but I found it romantic to think that one could say this through a science. This is why, as I see it, the other comes into play on a completely different level — the level, that is, of the conversation and not in relation to a social-political goal. I was, however, quite pleased with the fact that he at least hadn't done this for our philosophical journal but had only reported on the literature and engaged in critique without pursuing a political goal.

D.: So his misjudgment would have been to believe that science could solve these problems, that science could reach these goals, in which case he would only have to reach out to the citizenry and not to humanity as such?

G.: Yes, but he reached only a part of the citizenry or the public sphere. He didn't even reach the academic youth. Although it was quite estimable of him, wasn't it, that, when the '68 affair blew up, he didn't place himself blindly on the student side, but had the courage call them "left-fascists." The phrase is his, by the way. He was generally very talented in coining politically effective catchphrases like this expression, "left-fascism." In the meantime, we clearly saw how it had to end. It's quite clear that one cannot make a revolution with the students and leave the workers in peace. That, of course, couldn't work. I remember this period very clearly as the thing blew up and some of our colleagues who were actually interested in it said, "It wouldn't surprise me now if the students exploded. . . . "

D.: So Habermas also understood that it couldn't work?

G.: Yes, of course. His view of reality generally allowed him to see that things don't work like that. In the first place, they were intellectuals and, to that extent, not really such bad people at all. But they also were intellectuals who thought they could speak to the people or the labor force, and they were quite arrogant. I also had some experience with them here in Heidelberg. I remember one story — I don't know whether you were around then. . . .

D.: Yes, I was here at that time.

G.: Once, as I came into the lecture hall to give a talk, a girl stood on the lectern and said she had come there from the student body to report that the students had decided to strike. And so I said, "Oh yes? That's interesting, and now, no doubt, you'd like to tell my students who you work for!" Then the whole lecture hall started laughing, and she turned around and left.

D.: If we could turn away now from the protest movement and its failure (which Habermas himself realized) do you think that he had deceived himself about the possibility of science getting a grip on social problems, and that this is why it didn't affect the public sphere?

G.: He really believed that one had to come to social reforms by way of science, and I have always thought that it wouldn't work that way. What we need, if I may express it this way, is, in a certain sense, to win the great mass of the population back toward a sense of the state. This was what we needed then and even what we actually had, in a way, among the middle classes. We certainly had plenty of citizens, but the gaping discord we were dealing with was the one we stepped into between "the proletariat" and "the bourgeoisie." What we needed now, after the debacle of communism, was, if we may call it this, the "bourgeoisification" of the workforce. And this is what happened — workers came to be so well paid that one could no longer call them the proletariat.

D.: And in your opinion how did that come about?

G.: Well, I would say that the need to dismantle the antagonism of the classes was naturally there on both sides. But this was done violently in the GDR [German Democratic Republic]. The SPD [German Social Democratic Party] was incorporated violently — all of the members of the SPD became communists by law. It even worked, in a manner of speaking. In this case, the proletariat wasn't brought around gradually to the idea of the tendency that was developing toward that thriving economy that the school of Ludwig Erhard and Walter Eucken had built up. Too bad it never occurred to Walter Ulbricht that one could reach the goal of eliminating poverty in this way — and with a success that we shouldn't deny entirely, because now the United States cannot keep up with us in this regard.

D.: So you think that one needs this "bourgeoisification" of the proletariat in order to bring the proletariat to it own self-awareness?

G.: But the fact that it received a better wage and, consequently, better living conditions came about by itself. Today, we are barely still aware of the fact that the proletariat had vented their rage at the rich in the old proletarian style. In its own way, America has avoided this also. But America did it in an economically cruel way in that it allowed the poor to become poorer and fall into poverty. In our case, the fact that we can no longer pay has now become more critical, and all of the speculation about a free East Asia will probably not come to a quick fruition.

D.: What will no longer be paid?

G.: One can no longer pay the students — it doesn't work any more. There's a great deal of speculation about it — right away everyone screams. One can understand this because it amounts to a new depression, which is getting worse. On the other hand, one must say that, as long as the fathers and the working families are paid decently, it does still work. I studied it very closely myself when I was the rector in Leipzig. There I had to offer a justification to the Russians for every single reason for admitting a student. And when it came to professors, it was nearly hopeless.

D.: I believe that during your time in Leipzig you wrote an essay about the working students. What were you trying to convey in the essay?

G.: I just thought that one could decide the question by diversifying the benefits of public education and training. In reality, there were no so-called "worker-students," as they were called then. I grasped this very quickly, and so I insisted on writing about it. It wasn't the working-class children who were proposed for admission into the university — it was always the most intellectual of the workers themselves.

D.: So in the GDR it was just like it was with us during the student movement — the student leaders were just intellectuals and had nothing to do with the workers at all?

G.: Yes, they were called workers there as well, but they weren't really workers. They were really sons of the middle class who had gotten fed up with high school because they hadn't gotten beyond puberty and so they went into the factories at fifteen or sixteen years of age. So these people were the "worker-students." God forbid, of course, that anyone be allowed to say out loud who they really were, which would have been an appalling cosmopolitanizing — but I was aware of it.

D.: So they were accepted into the university because they were so-called workers — or because one called them that?

G.: Yes, exactly. Now, the kind of privileges that one enjoys through one's family and its social standing has always been rewarded. But what is more important is what one can do in reality and not in the abstract to make it so that these privileges are not so decisive. The elimination of the classes, which, practically speaking, has already occurred here in Germany, was quite important in this regard — very much in contrast to Italy. Italy still hasn't quite overcome this problem.

D.: Not in southern Italy, anyway. In northern Italy it's perhaps more like it is in Germany. There are also differences in northern Italy — for example, between the eastern and the western sides of Italy. Venice, Lombardy, and Emilia-Romagna are the richest regions now. Not only is there no unemployment, to the contrary, every possible foreign worker from the Slavic countries of Slovenia, Croatia, and Albania and northern Africa comes there.

G.: Now, the question of unemployment is the crucial question for everything that we've done until now. It has yet to be solved. What they've done in America is actually possible — that is, to offer so little support to the impoverished. But something we can do (which is what the Americans precisely did do) is to organize the unions internally — within the company. In an automobile company that's making good money, the wages are not decided through a bureaucratic parliamentary trade union commission. Instead, if the company has earned a lot, then the wages have to be higher, and they likewise have to be lowered if they themselves see that they aren't competitive. I think this difference in the American form of labor is exemplary. We must also establish this kind of union. It does, of course, create new kinds of responsibility for individuals. I can't really judge it — I'm not sufficiently trained in economics — but I have learned a great deal from observing the development of the two countries. They already have a multitude of things today that we would probable do well to adopt here immediately. Trying to negotiate for everyone through one office and through people who are paid from the money of the workers just doesn't work. And our workers don't really negotiate either — they have nothing to say about it. Everything is delegated. Our entire political system is completely bureaucratized. I'm also very critical of our electoral system. It's utterly in need of reform along the lines of America or England. We have to go back to the idea that only those people elected in a district can form a party and not those nominated from a list in some office in such way that everything gets decided within the party. I'm only talking now about the SPD.

American social democracy works much better in that, first of all, it has localized wage adjustments or wage disputes; and, second, the electoral system is also localized. I can't judge whether something like that would be possible in our case. These are problems that are beyond my comprehension. But I can see that whatever is achieved in this way a stronger accommodation between economics and politics has to result. I would say that both of them have to transform themselves. The first point, then, is that wage disputes must be localized; the second is to have genuine parliamentary rolls that are local so that one knows the parliamentarians in one's area. I have gradually come to connect these two points on the basis of my long experience — and wherever this is achieved one also has a tighter relationship between economics and politics.

D.: If we come back now to our theme of your confrontation with Habermas (which took place during this time), what would you say to bring this confrontation to a conclusion?

G.: What I now respect about Habermas is, first of all, that the same rules essentially apply to both of us — whatever I didn't understand about him, he didn't understand about me. I didn't understand anything about him. Nevertheless, I would still say that I discovered in him a very respectable and humane willingness to learn. I think the tremendous thing about the experience I had with Habermas is that our attempt at a conversation has shown us both that we must learn from each other and that the arguments that we each brought into the discussion weren't pushed further simply because they came from the other person, but, rather, we gave as good as we got. He was unable to make a political person out of me; I was unable to make a philosophical person out of him — he has remained a political thinker. I wouldn't say that I have no political talent — I have perhaps been able to show it, although in entirely different circumstances. I did display it as rector in Leipzig. In fact I probably have my talent for political diplomacy to thank for the fact that I got out of there intact, as a leftover from the Third Reich, as the one responsible for hindering [the development of] the "People's" University of Leipzig.[4] But the entire situation has turned itself around there. I recently received an honorary doctorate from there — although, in the meantime, their teaching has deteriorated.

---

4. [Gadamer is presumably referring to his efforts to deter the Communists from asserting complete ideological control over the University of Leipzig during his tenure as rector there in 1947.]

D.: Wouldn't you say that the philosophical bases of Habermas' universal pragmatism and of your hermeneutic dialogue are essentially the same?

G.: I only know that in his initial commentary he took an unbiased look at my outlines and errors and has begun to express himself much more cautiously, and I know in particular that the personal relationship between us no longer has any difficulties at all. But I would still say that he is essentially not a philosopher. He's essentially a political thinker.

D.: At this point we can bring our initial question to conclusion by asking, once again, does politics have nothing to do with philosophy and does philosophy have nothing to do with politics? Or, better, what role does philosophy play in politics?

G.: In a given instance, of course, philosophy can exercise criticism. It can provide a great deal of criticism, but politics isn't something that one can achieve through scholarship. To my mind, this is why rhetoric is so important — but in the way that Plato saw it. It makes no sense to go into politics in order to change the world. The time has passed when a Pericles could come into power. One can offer advice, one can stand up for something concrete, but as a citizen, as a member of society — as a philosopher, one might as well say, "I am here to observe the stars." For Plato, politics is the product of a declining democracy not an aspiring one. In the end, he's only trying to give us advice by pointing out what is grotesque about a democracy. The *Republic* was written for a Syracusan, not for an Athenian.

7

Tradition and Emancipation

D.: Habermas has accused you of conservativism in that he sees the focus of hermeneutics as being directed primarily at the tradition, which would simply legitimize authority. Tradition would be the prevailing power in the society or the state, and it would therefore be inclined to authoritarianism. As opposed to this, the critical reflection of German Idealism has taught us to dissolve the inherent nature of society and state through the anticipation of true life. What do you think of this accusation?

G.: Of course, I am perfectly willing to admit that my generation grew up under authoritarian conditions, but I would also say that it learned a great deal. That is to say, I belong to the generation that still remembers the estate system of the old Prussian state [*der Ständesstaat*]. When I was child in Prussia there was even still a right to vote that worked according to income — an election based on three class. At the time, my father, being a chemist and a university professor, had a high salary and income, and on election day in the region in which we lived in Breslau, he came home and said, "It was very important for me to be there. In fact, I tipped the balance — I was ranked number three in the upper class." He never was very far to the right — before the Weimar Republic he was always a National Liberal.

D.: At that time, then, one voted according to one's estate or class?

G.: Yes. Admittedly, I no longer remember exactly how it worked. It was during my childhood. But, obviously, we hung on every word of what my father said when he came home, satisfied because he had done well and thinking, "I was ranked third." The upper class was quite small.

D.: The upper class was perhaps the class of the landowners?

G.: No, no — it was the class of the highest officials, like my father. There was Herr Niesser, who was a professor and a merchant as well — much wealthier, of course, than my father. Lacking a family fortune, my father was wealthy only [because of the salary he received] through his institution. We even lived quite thriftily in a castle that you can see now in prints — it was very beautiful, quite dreamlike.

D.: Wasn't it expensive to live there?

G.: Not at all! No, the house would have been absolutely uninhabitable if we hadn't paid for a staff. There was no central heating, just two very large stoves. I didn't even know until the outbreak of the war what we did in the winter to keep it so nice and warm. The gardener came early in the morning and lit the two stoves, and so as the day began it was equally warm everywhere, and that was sufficient until evening. So it was only indirectly expensive to live there. The rent, of course, wasn't expensive — who else would have lived there? Only someone who had the money to pay the staff could live there. So we had two servants and a gardener. Without them it wouldn't have worked. We couldn't have lived there otherwise.

Thank God I earned my doctorate at a very young age! One either does one's doctoral work too early or too late. Otherwise it doesn't get done at all! (Gadamer laughs.) In any case, that's how it can be. So in my case it was very clear what I had to do. I had to convince my father that if he kept giving me so many botany books, zoology books, and the like on my birthday it wouldn't accomplish anything — I had no interest in it. I really wanted to go the theater and read Shakespeare, and so on. During the war we could no longer light all the stoves. So all of a sudden my study was moved into the large dining hall, and he saw the things I was reading lying there. The fact that it was Shakespeare was very distressing for him!

D.: In your opinion, was the society in which you grew up an authoritarian society or not?

G.: It was mostly a militaristic society. (I didn't make myself clear.) My teachers in school were all reserve officers. One referred to them as the "volunteers." Do you know what they were?

D.: No, I don't.

G.: Well, that was when you did the "one-year,"[1] which was the lower fifth. If you did military service as a so-called volunteer, then you no longer needed two years in the military but just a year if you had taken the *Abitur*[2] — or even if you hadn't taken it. In any case, it was just one year — that was the real goal. And so they even excused working-class children from a few years of school sometimes in order to create the one-year, as they called it. Ever since my childhood the term "one-year" has been as self-evident to me as any familiar word you can mention today. These people who had done the one-year could then be called up to the military at any time, as they can today in Switzerland. If a person subsequently became a teacher, then he would still be favored while teaching.

D.: So military training was important for becoming a teacher.

G.: The teachers were all reserve officers. And when the war broke out... suddenly, all of the teachers were at the front, and we got frightful old pedants as teachers. Though not always — in one case I had a magnificent Greek teacher. So half a year after 1914, the war had broken out, and all the teachers were having to go to the front — and they weren't coming back. Now, what I was trying to say was that this was really how militarism proliferated. We were in a good school, a very good school. Bavaria couldn't keep up with us then — at that time, anyone who came to high school in Silesia from Bavaria or from northern Germany had to go back at least one grade. So in our case the school was very good — with certain limitations, of course. Then, when the war came, along came the old rattle-traps. But we did get this one very good Greek teacher. In fact, the reason I became a classical philologist was that Heidegger could see that I was very good at Greek (even if I hadn't learned anything).

1. [*Das Einjährige* is the lower school-leaving certificate, which was originally the standard required for one-year volunteers.]
2. [*Das Abitur* is the school-leaving examination required for admission to university.]

D.: So it was an authoritarian and militarized society. Was Habermas correct, then, when he took you for a product of that conservativism and militarism?

G.: Yes, it was a militarized society — it was obviously so. As I lived through 1913 as a boy — I was thirteen years old then — all the newspapers were full of the Napoleonic Battle in Leipzig,[3] and it was all depicted quite objectively — how many mercenaries there were, how many had fallen....I even experienced this militarism in one geography lesson, when the teacher came to talk about Togo and said, "Yes, it is a tiny colony, and at the next opportunity we will stick this one in our pocket too." The teacher who made this remark during the geography lesson was, of course, a colonial officer.

D.: Is Habermas correct, then, when he says that you come from an authoritarian society?

G.: Of course, how it could be otherwise? That's just how it was. But I'd appreciate it if you would let me present my case: The liberation came in 1918, and the fact that I was reading Shakespeare instead of botany or zoology books was already a sign of new things....

D.: Really? How did it come to that?

G.: I'm trying to tell to you how I escaped the prevailing militarism in spite of everything. This wasn't anything special or new. With very rare exceptions, of course, all of my relatives were reserve officers — that's why there was an upper middle class at all. As I said, the bad thing about it was that before 1918 we got nothing but very old case-hardened pedants in many departments. This was certainly the case in the basic subjects. Learning Greek, of course, was a special desire of mine, and it was better there. But the ideological indoctrination that was supposed to go with it was completely antiquated. May I mention one example of it? We were reading Herodotus (or it was Thucydides? I do not remember exactly, but I believe it was Herodotus), who described the Spartan upbringing and the fact that it was normal for boys and girls to participate in sports together, naked. "Was this good?" was the question. We had to learn to say, "No!" That's how it was — it was such an outmoded education that even the good teachers had to busy themselves with such moralistic pedantry. In

3. [In 1913 a monument was raised in Leipzig to commemorate the Prussian and allied victory over Napoleon, which was fought in Leipzig in October of 1813.]

any case, I liberated myself immediately at that point. Admittedly, the deciding factor for me was a book about Asia by Theodor Lessing that described precisely how all of this optimism about progress and efficiency, so to speak, was a completely one-sided orientation and relationship to the world and one that, in contrast to Confucianism and the fatalism of the other great Asiatic countries, represented a peculiar global superiority — the same global superiority, that is, that we now attribute to America when we say that America dominates the world.

D.: Was he right? Were you on his side?

G.: Of course he was right. This is why I decided for the rest of my life not to submit myself any further to this pathos of sheer accomplishment. Yes, I did liberate myself, and I wasn't the only one. Many of the other students I got to know were with me. It was something my parents wouldn't listen to, but as undergraduates we were enlightened by it. Theodor Lessing was absolutely right. He was right, that is, to critically disavow this shortcoming of the militaristic, capitalist society.

Then came the revolution, and then the elections, and I heard some prominent and extremely good speakers from all four parties during my first semester in Breslau. Every party nominated a good candidate.

D.: This was during the Weimar Republic?

G.: Just prior to the Republic, during the elections — or in preparation for the elections. No, this wasn't really for the elections, but rather for the political education of the student body. It was a student body event to which prominent professors were invited. We had one for the Marxists first, then one for the Social Democrats, one for the Liberals, and one for the Conservatives. I actually found them all quite even-handed about many things, and I remained undecided between the two last.

D.: Between the Liberals and Conservatives? Then Habermas is right in thinking that you come from a background of conservativism?

G.: Of course I did; but there is more to it than that. I subsequently came to Marburg, and who was it there who attracted me the most? Richard Hamann, and he was actually a Social Democrat.

D.: What was the difference between conservativism and liberalism?

G.: Conservativism was Kaiser-friendly, and liberalism was Kaiser-hostile!

D.: That was the only difference?

G.: "Only," you say? That is quite a lot! My father, who always associated with these reserve officers, was nevertheless quite critical of them.

D.: Was your father conservative or liberal?

G.: He wasn't conservative — oh no, Bismarck was his hero, not the second Wilhelm. My father was in Friedrichsruh with torch in hand in 1895 for Bismarck's eightieth birthday.[4] And that's why the other side — namely, the religious side, which occupied the other middle class districts — wasn't right for him. For him there was only Bismarck.

D.: So, given that you were enthused by all of them, you're saying that the candidates of the four parties said basically the same thing.

G.: Oh no, not the same thing. It's just that there was such a high quality among everyone there, among all four parties — though least of all among the Communists. The Social Democrat was the Baron von Biberstein or something like that. But the Liberal fascinated me the most. This was a professor of economics from Jena — an outstanding speaker. Something about his speech very much impressed that nineteen-year-old, and, from that moment on, I had someone to bolster me. Then, when I came to Marburg, I became liberated very quickly. So the kind of conservativism that Habermas is thinking of is utterly alien to me.

D.: But can one perhaps say that both conservatives and liberals had the same conception of authority — a conception that would lead to authoritarianism?

4. Friedrichsruh was Bismarck's residence from 1871 until his death in 1898. In 1871 Bismarck became chancellor and was allowed to acquire the former castle of Count Friedrich zur Lippe. It is situated in the Sachsenwald, near Lauenburg in Schleswig-Holstein. Bismarck operated out of Friedrichsruh until the time of his removal from office in 1890. In 1895 the Reichstag officially refused to send congratulations to Bismarck on his eightieth birthday. This resulted in regular pilgrimages to Friedrichsruh that took on the characteristics of saint worship — hence the torches. (Source: Brockhaus)

G.: No, not at all. His mistake was not to have understood that it isn't the concept of authority, it's the appeal to it that leads to authoritarianism. He just couldn't comprehend this. Inasmuch as authority is used as the basis of an argument, then that you have authoritarianism — but far be it from me to do that. Because he didn't understand this distinction at the time, at first he fell into the same mistake that the protest movement did, and he only wised up about it after this abortive experience.

D.: So there is one authority that comes from consensus and another authority that is just social coercion and power?

G.: More precisely, there is one authority that is just social coercion and one that comes from proper decision making.

D.: And that one would be a recognized authority?

G.: Yes, but not just recognized. To come back to the previous point, liberals were those who defended their counter-position against the hard-line conservatives, the empire, and militarism. Along with all the German nationalists, the patriotic types, the progressives, and so on, my father was also against the hard-liners. But Bismarck was something different. If Bismarck hadn't been dismissed from office by his Kaiser, world history would have been different. Then there wouldn't have been a First World War. The war was due to an inability to conduct a sensible foreign policy on this soil. Austria — with the assassination of Archduke Ferdinand in the Balkans — also belonged in this context. They could bring about a global catastrophe again at any time.

D.: Would Bismarck, then, be an authentic example of a recognized authority?

G.: He was one example — primarily through his independence from what Wilhelm II was preparing to do at that time with overwhelming force, which ultimately resulted in a blind military invasion.

D.: This, then, would be an example of the distinction between authority and power, in Latin between *auctoritas* and *potestas*. Habermas wasn't aware of this distinction at the time.

G.: Yes, I suppose not — or perhaps he thought I knew this all along. That could also be it. But, in any case, he misunderstood me at the time so badly that it actually became an outright defeat for him. I

remember in great detail how at one point we had an evening symposium in Mannheim during which he accosted me, invoking the themes
of authority, tradition equaling power, and so forth — and there were
many others (among them even my students, like Volkmann-Schluck,
for example) who didn't get it right away either. But, in the end, I
pulled off a brilliant victory by telling him, "You've got the most crucial thing backwards. It isn't about admitting what comes from the
tradition to be true but of forming a judgment by oneself." But it was
rather impressive of Habermas that he wasn't obstinate about it and
he did, after all, concede a certain authority to me. He, of course, was
convinced that indoctrination was patently wrong. It really would
have been something if Habermas himself had been a thoroughgoing
conservative. Like him, I didn't read the newspapers that came to the
house; instead, I read the ones that the working men read.

D.: What do you mean when you say you pulled off a victory that
evening?

G.: That, in the end, one thing actually became clear to him — in
spite of being at the limit of his understanding. Now I don't think of
him as a revolutionary but as a critic, which is what the liberals were.

D.: But what about Heidegger? On which side would he have been —
on side of the liberals or the conservatives?

G.: That's very hard to say. He was certainly no militarist.

D.: Although he did, at one time, have an admiration for the military,
didn't he? Wasn't he even in the First World War?

G.: No, in the Second.

D.: But he was also called up to be a soldier in the First World War.
He was called up very shortly at the end of the Second World War as
well, when the French had already come across the border, and they
were supposed to defend Freiburg with the reserves.

G.: Yes, but this experience didn't have any significance for him at
all. Yes, he was also in the First World War — that's correct, but
only very shortly. He had a heart attack, and so he was immediately
discharged. But let's not talk about that — people have talked too
much about his private life.

D.: Wasn't his wife, who later led him into National Socialism, originally a liberal and even participated in the first feminist movement?

G.: Even worse than that, she was a Guelph. Do you know what that is? In 1866, after the German-Austrian war, which signaled the end of Prussia and led to the foundation of the German Empire, the Guelphs were the ones who opposed the Empire. The provinces of Hanover and Northern Germany wanted to remain English (the king of England was, at the same time, the king of Hanover). And throughout the 1870 war there was a very tense situation among the militaries. Only the diplomatic talent of Bismarck during the second war made it possible for them to enter into the federation (as did the southern German states), and the foundation of the German Empire of the Kaisers arose from this — including the special laws that one still sees in Bavaria. For there had always been borders — there was even a period when there were borders between the states. Now, the Guelphs are those who never recognized this compulsory incorporation into a Prussian entity; my wife, for example, was a Guelph — an avid one. So a Guelph rejected this kind of Prussian militarism and conventionalism and conservativism and so on. They saw it as coercion. These people were referred to by the famous medieval term, Guelphs, because they offered resistance and had their own party in the Reichstag. This was Westphalia, the inhabitants of Westphalia. She came from there. And, for her, anything that came out of Prussia was wrong.

D.: If Heidegger's wife also belonged to this party, then is what Hermann Mörchen reports and what Safransky takes up again in his Heidegger biography incorrect — that is, that she crossed over from her original liberalism to National Socialism and that her husband followed her?

G.: On the contrary, he was the one who did that. Furthermore, she was a genuine wife who — as was proper at the time — followed the will of her husband unfailingly. This is absolutely certain. She was, however, quite tactless, and that could also be misunderstood. There is one particular episode that was described to me and that I have no reason to doubt. There was an assistant of Heidegger's who was also a Jew; and on one occasion Frau Heidegger made several anti-Semitic remarks. Consequently, he went to Heidegger one evening and said to him, "You should know that I am Jew, and if you want to get rid of me, then please do." Heidegger shook his hand and said, "That really changes nothing between us." So, he was not an anti-Semite.

D.: But was his wife an anti-Semite?

G.: God, no — that would be going too far. She just gossiped with everyone — she was a clever woman. But neither should you discount the role of the middle class — they shouldn't be completely absolved of all this. When it comes to anti-Semitism, the main thing is to view the matter quite soberly from the outset. You have to see what I was able to see quite well, particularly in Silesia, as a continuous stream of immigration of very highly talented Jewish people came from the East — especially from Poland and Russia. It was an enormous flood, and it propagated a certain anxiety rather than an antipathy toward them. I had many Jewish friends, and they were the first to say to me, "Listen, how long can this go on?" One even said to me, "I heard that the *chargé d'affaires* of the foreign ministry was a Zionist. That will turn out very badly for us." In fact, it was Jakob Klein who said to me, "We will have an anti-Semitic persecution because of this" — or a staged one, at least, because one always could count on that in those days.

D.: So, was this scholar of the mathematics and logistics of Greek thinking a Jew, and was he your friend?

G.: Of course he was a Jew, and so were Leo Strauss and Löwith and all my fellow students and colleagues in Marburg. And I was friends with all of them, thank God. So I never fell in with Hitler for a single moment because I told myself that it wasn't even an option for me to vote for someone who was an anti-Semite. Anti-Semitism was too repugnant a position to take because it speaks only to the worst side of human nature.

D.: And Frau Heidegger? Didn't she take part in anti-Semitism to some extent, even though she was a Guelph?

G.: At most, she gossiped with people about it. In one respect we were really the same — I never behaved ambiguously during that time. In any case, she defended me whenever Heidegger claimed that I was ruining his philosophical project. Not just me, of course, but any philosopher. He was constantly associating with the Nazis, and everyone thought he was crazy. As he was foundering, the only re-action that was possible for him was to scold us — he was deeply

disillusioned. Although he *was* decent enough to give up the rectorship after three-quarters of a year. And, I'm sorry, but it would be
hard to find anyone else who would give up a rectorship voluntarily
after three-quarters of a year. So people really do a gross injustice to
Heidegger by not taking this into account — it ought to mean something when one won't put up with the rectorship for the minimum
tenure of one year and actually steps down before then. The things
other people are concerned about — his denunciation of a colleague
and the like — I am convinced that he should perhaps have been more
cautious in these matters, because in such cases one can be taken in
by every word. I mean, I must say (albeit from my own experience)
how unspeakably stupid a world full of spies and so forth is. I think
I told you a few of the stories from the time when I was in Leipzig.

D.: When you were the rector in Leipzig?

G.: No, when I was a professor there, not rector, and the Nazis were
still in power. You must understand that during that period one denunciation would come after another, and in my opinion it was pure
idiocy — it didn't pay to take it too seriously. But one time a real
denunciation did come along. A student wrote about my seminar to
her girlfriend who was not there that semester: "I was with Gadamer
today. Can you believe he actually said, 'All asses are brown?' " Now,
the girl to whom the letter was written was from a family with Nazi
parents. She left the letter lying around, the parents saw it, read it,
and I was reported to the rector. So I was asked to go to the rector,
who was no Nazi sympathizer (no more than I was) but . . . he said to
me, "So, my dear colleague, how did come to speak out against the
Brown-shirts by saying, 'All asses are brown'? What did you meant by
that?" "You don't understand," I replied, "I was merely explaining
the first premise of an Aristotelian syllogism with the famous medieval example, 'All asses are brown; Brunellus is an ass; therefore,
Brunellus is brown.' For medieval philosophers, all asses are brown,
and Brunellus is the name of an ass that they often used." So the rector wrote into the record, "Professor Gadamer was merely explaining
the first premise of a syllogism using a medieval example." The rector
and I were of similar minds, and there were very few Nazis in Leipzig
anyway. The center of the anti-Nazi resistance, the famous Church
of St. Thomas (which you can still visit today), was there. There were
even some small anti-Nazi posters put up there.

D.: Didn't the Nazis know this, and didn't they do anything about it?

G.: The church — especially the Catholic Church — was protected by the army. Everyone knows that the army always needs the aid and solace of the church for casualties and for the soldiers themselves. The concordat still served this purpose, but, of course, it couldn't go beyond certain limits because one could be accused of the political exploitation of Catholicism.

D.: So there was a law according to which one could be accused of political Catholicism?

G.: Yes, there was such a law. The political exploitation of Catholicism was punishable.

D.: Why? Because National Socialism thought that the church was too powerful?

G.: Yes, of course. The concordat was a compromise by both sides. They used all of the old wives' tales about things that happen in the church against the church. Later, they even put a famous Protestant theologian on trial within the Protestant Church. But there were also trials because of embarrassing stories of things that were happening in the Protestant Church. Internally, every church has its embarrassing stories about things of a sexual nature — even in Italy, of course (Gadamer smiles). These trials against clergymen accused of such things were resolved by the concordat, in effect blackmailing whoever could be identified through these falsehoods, through these stories. But there was now an amnesty for the violators. The amnesty was in place, but one could still be accused of the political exploitation of Catholicism. I was rather naive then. I didn't have a clue about what was going on, but I had a friend who explained it to me — a Protestant colleague, a clergyman from southern Germany.

D.: Let's get back now to the problem of anti-Semitism with which we began and which you said was a phenomenon that we must reflect upon impartially at first. You spoke of the responsibility of the middle classes, whom we cannot completely excuse, and of the rivalry that arose among the educated strata of society, and the fear that arises in the population every time a large-scale immigration into Germany occurs. Could you tell us something more about that? Is it the same

immigration problem that we still have today and the correspond-
ingly difficult situation of the minorities and the problems that they
pose for their adopted country?

G.: I have very often had to grapple with this topic, and I think we
are dealing here with very difficult events. We can't delude ourselves
about the fact that the members of a minority (even when we aren't
talking about Jews) always stick blindly to their minority group. My
father was in the habit of saying, "I have nothing against Jews. One or
two colleagues — very well; but we can't tolerate three colleagues any
more, because then we won't get any more non-Jews at our university." For the most part, he was correct. Marburg was just such a case.
We had many Jews there, and they were all good people. Auerbach
was a Jew, and I didn't see any misfortune in that at all. Erich Frank
was also a Jew. The philosophers Jakob Klein, Löwith, Leo Strauss
were all Jews, as were Jacobsthal, the archeologist, Jakobsohn, the
linguist, and so on.

D.: Jakobsohn, the famous linguist, was in Marburg as well, and he
was also a Jew?

G.: Yes, of course. All of them were in Marburg. The only exception
was in the natural sciences — there were others there as well. But in
our case, the logic went like this: If there were already three Jews
present then no one else came, except for more Jews. But this is true,
of course, not just for the Jews, but for every minority. It's the norm,
and it keeps every minority together. And that's why the opposition
from those who are disturbed by it is just as egoistic. That's also
why it has little to do with the overblown rhetoric that people use in
connection with it. I do admit, of course, that it's unjust to oppose
minorities, and whenever it falls into the hands of the masses and
the mass media it can get very nasty. You know that I experienced
Kristallnacht. . . .

D.: Did you really? What kind of impression did it make on you?

G.: I was in Marburg, living in a very modest house. Above me was a
lower middle class family who were very nice people and who raised
the insects and butterflies from which silk is made. The husband had
the machines necessary to produce the silk from them. So he lived
above us, and we had a very friendly relationship. His first wife had
many talents, and she was extremely attractive and very sociable.

It was just that she didn't take care of their child very much, and so in his second marriage she was replaced by this young woman. Well, she was a friendly woman, and she came home one evening and shouted in despair, "Herr Doktor" (I was already a doctor by then), "have you heard? They have set fire to the synagogue!" Every German, even this family, was outraged by this theatrical, vandalistic display of fanaticism. I'm still utterly convinced that it was a crass and frightful display.

D.: And how were things, then, with your Jewish friends? What became of them?

G.: As I said, I had genuine Jewish friends long before the whole thing started in 1933. First Löwith and then Jacobsthal, the archeologist, and Erich Frank, the philosopher, and Auerbach, who was a good friend of mine, and so on — they were all Jews. I had an old student friend, Jakob Klein. He lived in Berlin among a small circle of friends with whom he pursued philosophy. And, of course, this disappeared the moment Hitler make his power grab. He subsequently came to see me, and I invited him to live with me; and so he spent his last two years in Germany living with me. He lived, as it were, under the table! This wasn't so difficult either — people are just too stupid. If I were simply to begin recounting right now how I managed to become a full professor without ever joining the party, I could put it quite succinctly — I read Machiavelli. Machiavelli says, "The enemies of my enemy are my close friends." In accordance with this motto, then, I have repeatedly forgiven the people who joined the party with a bad conscience — unlike most people who, in their unfailing "bravery," would have nothing to do with them. No, in the beginning I tried to take such scholars seriously, and this is also how I later came to Leipzig (Gadamer grins amusedly). I didn't really do it in a calculated manner — I did it quite naturally. Now, I was friends with Bultmann at the time as well, and that also helped me because he had a very considerable reputation as a theologian. All of this helped me not only to come to Leipzig as a full professor, but also to support and assist my friend Jakob Klein.

8

Philosophy in
the Eye of the Storm

D.: How, then, was it possible? How could it happen against the will of the overwhelming majority of the population?

G.: On the one hand were ignorance and the fact that no one ever would have considered anything like that possible. On the other hand there was...militarism, which is perhaps too crude a word, and yet, all in all, something like that. Someone who is accustomed to obeying orders doesn't sanction them, he just carries them out. That's really the essence of obedience. And it's what now makes me so enormously pensive. And, in a deeper sense, aren't we really accomplices to it all? I don't mean me or my generation—I mean world history. How could world history happen like this only in Germany—in a Germany that produced a very high level of theology on both sides, in spite of all the discord between Catholicism and Protestantism? Because theology cannot occur otherwise. And, moreover, it inevitably produces dissension, strife.

D.: But, how was it possible that something like that happened in Germany, in a Germany that had reached such a high intellectual plateau?

G.: Indeed, how it was possible? How was it possible that the generals didn't see what would happen to Germany after the Röhm putsch and the Night of the Long Knives? And how was it possible that they could tolerate it? Schleicher was done away with—shot—and the journalists who had written the von Papen speech[1] were also gotten rid of, and so on. That's just how it was. Why, then—why did

1. [The speech delivered by former Reichs-chancellor von Papen to the University of Marburg on June 17, 1934, denouncing the Nazi suppression of freedom of the press and the church.]

we tolerate all of this? Perhaps because so many discharged officers were waiting for something new to come along, something like the *Wehrmacht,* which had the weapons, and in which they could now serve themselves and have a chance to grab new posts. That was the frightening thing, as I look back on it.

D.: So you believe that the *Wehrmacht* should have reacted after the Röhm putsch. But didn't Hitler carry out the Röhm putsch jointly with the German armed forces?

G.: No, he didn't carry it out jointly with the *Reichswehr,* but there was a pact. No, the putsch came about because he had his own people shot. The S.A. was disarmed — whether or not it was the *Reichswehr* is irrelevant.

D.: But the disarmament of the S.A. was carried out by the army.

G.: Perhaps that would still be possible even now — in fact, now more than ever. Take, for example, the Munich Agreement, which came about in the hope of concluding a peace — and then Hitler marched right into Prague. We can't deny that our leading generals threatened to step down — they didn't want to risk it. When, beyond all reason and logic, the war then took on such gigantic proportions, no one thought to settle the matter with a few well-aimed shots. And why not? That's the question we should be asking. Can one abolish despotism without violence? This was Goerdeler's failing. To the very end, he didn't want to do Hitler any harm — he just wanted to remove him from power. What kind of a thing is that? How could anyone think something like that? I don't know. We were all blind in some way or another. And when I awoke, so to speak, from this nightmare, I also asked myself how it was possible. In the beginning I had genuine Jewish friends in the area, and they all said, "Don't worry — that guy won't last more than a year." Among the intellectual middle class, everyone was completely convinced of this. Then, step-by-step, things escalated again and again — especially, of course, in the case of the merchants, the bankers, and the like, and their interests, but that doesn't make for a popular sentiment. No, no; I can see only one explanation — the old Prussian willingness to obey. It just continued to function. And I have to say that the fact that it did continue to function was very, very dangerous. And anyone could have seen what just one desperate officer, after four years of a wasted war, did see and finally tried to do something about — wasn't it Stauffenberg?

D.: But wasn't Stauffenberg a member of the Goerdeler conspiracy?

G.: No, not directly. Stauffenberg disagreed with the coup they were plotting. It was a desperate affair that he no longer wanted to go along with. Perhaps he had seen that (with people like Goerdeler in it, who didn't want to do Hitler any harm but only wanted to depose him) it could accomplish nothing in the end. It's quite possible that he himself was thinking, "We'll never be rid of him this way." Or perhaps someone suggested this to Stauffenberg. It was just too bad that his plot was so protracted and it only became possible at that moment. If it had happened prior to this, before the attack on Poland, at least half a year if not earlier — before we had to fight on our own fronts, Bohemia and Austria and so on . . . but it went on for years before anyone noticed what Stauffenberg had seen. Of course, we deceived ourselves once again when the Austrians in Vienna all yelled "Hurrah!" as the German forces invaded. The same thing then happened in the Tyrol and elsewhere. These were all dreadful weaknesses that we would have to pay for later.

D.: Do you think the *Wehrmacht* supported Hitler and went along with the Röhm putsch because it had been arranged that only the *Wehrmacht* would carried weapons after the disarmament of the S.A.?

G.: Certainly. On the other hand, it also prevented more severe civil strife.

D.: The S.A. was a large force, wasn't it? It was about three million people.

G.: They were really very determined people. Of course, few of the people in it were proper soldiers. And, of course, the *Reichswehr* wanted no one else to carry arms but themselves. That was certainly the reason why they ultimately supported the putsch and also why they swore allegiance to Hitler. They remained loyal to this oath to the end because of Prussian militarism and rigor, and this is why they no longer wished to eliminate Hitler. If they had seen things more keenly, then they would have backed Schleicher — and they shouldn't have allowed him to be liquidated by Hitler. If Schleicher hadn't waited, he would certainly have been the victor. But I have to confess, that's how it is with history — people often make the wrong decisions.

On the other hand, I do want to point out that anti-Semitism was completely unpopular among the people — there was no question of Germans desiring it.

D.: Did Jaspers, perhaps, think otherwise?

G.: No, not Jaspers. . . . I don't know — I didn't know him well enough. I wouldn't make the mistake of thinking he would say that. It was difficult for him because his students were so disappointed. And yet, looked at as a whole, he responded to the entire situation with enormous tact.

D.: Were the students disappointed because his wife was a Jew?

G.: Yes — although he wasn't one of their leaders. They were keenly aware of this by now, but he had sufficient noblesse to remain at his wife's side. I never once doubted that he would do that. There were some people at the time who separated from their wives.

D.: Yes, and many people suggested — and quite emphatically — that he should do it as well so he could free himself from this situation in order to resume his position at the university. He said this himself in a television interview on his seventy-fifth birthday. He also told how appalled he was when Heidegger was invited to Heidelberg in 1933 by the National Socialist Student Association, and he walked into the philosophy seminar with a German uniform and the Hitler salute. Jaspers sat in the front row during the lecture and didn't applaud. Afterwards, when Heidegger, as usual, came to dinner as Jaspers' guest, the atmosphere was very strained. And when Jaspers asked, "How you can believe in such an uncultured man as Hitler?" Heidegger answered, "Oh, culture has nothing to do with it, just look at what beautiful hands he has." For Jaspers, that was the end of the friendship. Do you think Jaspers took him for a committed Nazi and anti-Semite, or did he just think he was fooling himself?

G.: No. I think after a few years he saw that Heidegger had just been fooling himself, and I think he thought Heidegger understood this as well. Jaspers, of course, understood that Heidegger had been dreadfully taken in, for there's really no question about it — who wouldn't have thought this? And he never really took him for an anti-Semite at all. That would have been impossible after his history with Arendt, but even besides that — no, no, there's no question about it. In fact, it's quite clear that by "National Socialism" Heidegger never meant anything other than the "Industrial Revolution." He thought that, for Hitler, the whole of Nazism was always the Industrial Revolution.

D.: But what about Jaspers? Surely Heidegger only saw National Socialism as the Industrial Revolution after he gave up the rectorship. The reason why he was against it then was that he had begun to read Hölderlin and to talk about nihilism. And he held his famous lecture on Nietzsche's will to power and technology, by which he meant the will to the total subjugation of nature and the real. But how did Jaspers view National Socialism?

G.: I don't know what he thought. I'm afraid he limited himself to moralizing. But then, the inhuman way that anti-Semitism had now become so overblown, and the fact that no one resisted it. . . . I think what the latter entails — what was decisive — was what I correctly put into words after the *Reichswehr* joined with Hitler: "You can't talk to tanks." Do you understand what I mean? Admittedly, they did try to do something with the money from Bosch[2] — the assassination attempt by Stauffenberg is evidence of this. Of course, they just didn't succeed. Schleicher wasn't shot arbitrarily — it was obviously premeditated. Schleicher wanted to come to power some day. He was no idiot, after all, and he thought that he really could deal with the guy. Von Papen and others thought Hitler was a nonentity, but not him, not Schleicher — he was no nonentity. In one of his first speeches he spoke of fighting the cowardliness within every human being, and he was right.

D.: And wasn't the real putsch planned by Schleicher and not by Röhm, as Hitler wanted people to believe?

G.: No, no — that's not how it happened. Schleicher's moment hadn't yet arrived. He was still waiting. He thought the situation could become even more favorable. He said, "What more could possibly happen?" That was his mistake. He hadn't counted on two things — first, the fact that they would dismiss him and, second, that in the meantime thousands of discharged officers saw in Hitler the chance to resume their profession. I had a nephew who was in this exact situation, and he was searching for something. He even came to me in Leipzig, and I asked him what he would do here. He answered, "This

---

2. [Robert Bosch, owner and founder of the Bosch electronics company in Stuttgart, was an anti-Nazi financier; Carl Goerdeler became a nominal representative of the Bosch Industrial Group.]

and that..." and "I don't know." None of these discharged officers had anything, and now they had everything again. A thousand or so of these officers, of course, arranged the terms for the peace between Hitler and the army. And Hitler, of course, consented. These people just wanted war again. The general staff, however, didn't want this; they resigned when he carried things too far. They couldn't believe that Hitler would be so insane. It was no longer possible to keep a tight rein on him, so he took the next step alone. We don't know the details. We only know that, if Hitler hadn't taken the offensive, then Stalin would have. We now know that the Russians, at very great expense, had prepared an enormous army with highly technical equipment. That much was quite clear. We also thought that they were going to attack us anyway, and if the Americans weren't prepared to aid us we were going to have a series of Marxist states in Europe.

D.: There was even a Russian historian who recently demonstrated that, in spite of the Ribbentrop Pact, Stalin was still preparing for war — with the intention of introducing communism into Europe. He tried to prove that Hitler knew all of this and was therefore forced to attack, and that Stalin subsequently forced him into a suicidal attack because Germany couldn't fight on two fronts.

G.: This is common knowledge — and it's true. And it's something one has to consider, and what I was considering as well. And this is why I was so terribly agitated — because I said to myself, "We just now lost one war. And now we're fomenting war again? Isn't this enough — do we really want to lose another a war?"

D.: Even by that time, what Goerdeler and the *Reichswehr* wanted was still a possibility — a separate peace with the West, that is.

G.: One would gladly have settled for that — yes, yes, but that's just not how it worked out. It was only possible once the West desired it; they tried it through Sweden and in several other ways.

D.: There was a high-ranking officer in the Luftwaffe, Rudolf Hess, a deputy of Hitler's who flew to England and crashed. Though he never admitted it, one presumes that he was sent to England by Hitler himself in order to reach a cease-fire secretly.

G.: Yes, yes, there were many attempts, but they always miscarried. That is to say, one can't expect nations who fought for years and sacrificed human lives to conclude a peace all of a sudden as if nothing had happened.

D.: Thomas Mann was also against the separate peace, wasn't he? I read a speech that he gave in 1944 in America for an American radio station in which he completely rules out the separate peace with Germany and Hitler.

G.: But in our case the discussion has never been pressed that far. It is hard to say what people thought in our case. All in all, we have to say that world history ran its course just as it had to.

D.: And would the Stauffenberg assassination attempt have come too late then, even if it had succeeded?

G.: Yes, of course, even the plot by Goerdeler, who was a Christian and friend of mine in Leipzig. He was a good Christian who wanted no blood. He didn't want anyone to kill Hitler. He only wanted someone to remove him from the head of the army. No, no, he was much more childlike than one imagines. I do admit, however, that there was something rational in all of this — it was even initiated and financed by the industrialists.

D.: Financed? For Goerdeler?

G.: Yes, of course — Bosch, the industry, all of it.

D.: His idea was to remove Hitler and redraw the old borders of the Reich?

G.: Yes, of course, without a lot of sacrifices — which would have been part of it in any case — but, the point was to conclude a peace in spite of the others. But, then we would have had a thirty-year-long war instead. The Russians, you see, wouldn't have held back any longer; they wanted victory. Yes, and the idea that the Americans would have actually risked their army after that — that's really absurd. What we didn't see we can't know. But, in any case, one probably has to say that the border in such a peace or treaty might have turned out to the Elbe instead of where it is today. One has to admit these days, especially with reunification, that people (my wife, for instance) think that the East is hardly worth anything.

D.: Not even Danzig, then, or Pomerania, or Breslau?

G.: She has always been convinced of this. She has always told me that Germany ends at the Elbe, and she told me long before the war that not just eastern Prussia but also the entire Slavic region belonging to eastern Germany was never really part of Germany. No one, of course, wanted it to become Russian — certainly not. I only mean that, in essence, she had no interest in eastern Germany at all — it was foreign to her. In fact, the opposition to Prussia in southern and western Germany didn't just come along recently, with reunification — everyone had been aware of it for a long time. Whenever I would look into a family home, or whenever I listened to some of the stories my wife told, stories her father, who was a clever man, had occasionally told, what I heard was, "They're all Slavs." And the first thing he said to me in 1933 was, "There's going to be a war for lands we don't even care about." Everyone, of course, hoped that they would stop it in time.

D.: Everything he foresaw then, as well as everything that actually happened, should be regarded today as a reminder, an instructive reminder of what could still happen even today if we permit such things to happen. What lesson do you think we should draw from the dreadful experiences of this century?

G.: Today we are faced with the fact that we no longer have a single minority within our society, but rather a variety of minorities who presumably want to integrate themselves into the society and yet have a very strong sense of their own community. This is why we are faced with the problem of their coexistence within the society. On the one hand, this sense of community inhibits clashes between a minority and its adopted society, but, on the other hand, the problem is exacerbated because some conflicts do arise. This brings the adopted society, quite consciously, to the point of closing itself off from minorities, to the point of being against every immigrating minority and, ultimately, against immigration as such, since the members of this society feel threatened. But it's no longer possible in Europe, and especially in the developed societies, to close oneself of from immigration. On the one hand, this is because of the variation in customs, but primarily it's because of the pressure on industrialized society to succeed in lowering the birth rate. In thirty or fifty years perhaps there will no longer even be "Germans" or "Italians" like there were before. So the problem of resolving the conflict between minorities and their adopted society as well as the conflicts among the minorities themselves is an unavoidable one.

D.: That does seem to be the task for society in the future, but on what basis can such a task be carried out?

G.: I don't know whether this conflict can be resolved simply on the basis of a constitutional state alone — particularly if communities arise that are composed of minorities who bring with them their own customs and traditions that are entirely different and come into conflict with one another. This is why I believe, once again, that only a dialogue among the different world religions can lead to mutual tolerance and respect and bring these minorities together — minorities who are really constituted on the basis of their religions. In Europe, just as in the rest of the world, only such a dialogue could lead to peaceful coexistence and mutual respect. In my book *Das Erbe Europas,* I have already shown that the real foundation of European civilization and its great cultural heritage consists precisely in this sense of tolerance. It took centuries fraught with wars and struggles for this idea of tolerance to establish itself. And, at the end of the eighteenth century — the century of the Enlightenment — it gave us Maria Theresa of Hapsburg's Edict of Tolerance, which did not arise on the basis of a simplistic rejection of all religions, but rather on the basis of their awareness of the strength of their own integral cultural identity. This strength is precisely what allows us neither to fear nor reject minorities and cultural differences, but rather to accept them. For we have the underlying certainty that our own integrity cannot be minimized in this mutual conversation — but neither will it simply dominate. It can serve, instead, as a basis for mutual understanding and respect. What essentially holds society together is this conversation itself.

9

Between Heidegger and Jaspers

D.: Let's come now to your relationship to Jaspers. How did you get to know him, and how did this relationship develop?

G.: I remember very clearly how Jaspers came into my purview. It was as a student when another student told me that there were some really interesting philosophical seminars going on in Heidelberg. The student was in Marburg, and he told to me about Jaspers. I took note of this with interest. Then I went to see Heidegger for the first time in Freiburg, and he heard that I was driving back to Marburg via Heidelberg. There were interruptions during the semester because of the French invasion, and Heidegger said to me, "Please be sure to visit Jaspers." So I said goodbye to him in Freiburg, and he said, "You're going to Heidelberg? Wonderful! Then please go see Rickert and send him my regards." So I did both. Rickert was a full professor of philosophy in Heidelberg, as was Jaspers, but he came from psychology. So I came back from Freiburg to Marburg, stopping in Heidelberg to visit Jaspers. I still remember it vividly — Jaspers really impressed me, though I felt like I was under psychoanalytic observation. Rickert, on the other hand, didn't see me at all because he just stared at the tops of his shoes the whole time. It was really pathetic.

D.: Let's come back to Jaspers. So he was also a medical doctor?

G.: Yes, he was a doctor. And, in a manner of speaking, he was a gentleman from a good family with money — and he was such a terribly fastidious person. I really never saw anything like it. But Heidegger kept extolling Jaspers' virtues, even with one quite beautiful expression: "He has a peculiar elegance in his manner," which means, "I have very little to do with him, but he impresses me." So

Heidegger really behaved ambivalently toward him, and so, in fact, did the Third Reich. Of course, nobody here remembers this, but when Heidegger took over the rectorship we were thunderstruck. Had he gone mad? Not one of my students could comprehended it, to say nothing of my friends. How could one even begin to grasp this? Then it went even further — on top of everything else, Heidegger became a Nazi. The same commotion in Heidelberg: "Frau Jaspers is a Jew. It's appalling," Jaspers' friends here in Heidelberg commented — friends who were themselves future Nazis. It was perfectly disastrous for them. Then along came some *nobody*[1] who ran things here (in Jaspers' district). I don't remember exactly what he was called. I only know that I received a letter from him when I was in Leipzig.

D.: From Jaspers?

G.: No, from this anonymous gentleman. Jaspers had already been in retirement for a long time, but I visited him regularly, which was all you could do. If you had a little intelligence, you could behave like a human being. And, of course, you didn't have to treat people who had become Nazis with a bad conscience by kicking them when they were down. You needed to show them some compassion, and that's what I did. I didn't condemn anyone who said to me, "You know I have a family. . . . What am I supposed to do?"

D.: Did you visit Jaspers because you knew he was having difficulties — that is, to stand by him in his circumstances?

G.: Yes, of course. I visited him regularly because his situation was clear to me and also because I felt overwhelmed by events. When Poland and France were occupied in 1940 (after the Hitler-Stalin Pact) I went to Jaspers and asked him, "Are we now facing a thirty-year-long war?" He nodded and said to me, "Well, Herr Gadamer, you know one can never predict history." Hitler, in fact, marched into the Balkans right after that. From that point on, we all knew that the war with Russia was coming and that would mean the end for Germany.

D.: And what was in the letter from this man who ran things in Heidelberg?

1. [Gadamer uses the English word "nobody" here.]

G.: It was Roßmann! You know, he later became Jaspers' successor in Basel. Nothing counted with him at all — not the fact that Jaspers had been through all of these things, not the fact that, as early as 1935, I had regularly tried to offer him a leg up. I actually found it quite nice that people here in Heidelberg greeted me anonymously! Anyway, I think I told you how it ended. When he was supposed to receive his honorary doctorate, I was right here at the time, and my friend Schaefer, the ancient historian, was dean. A very decent colleague from the university said to me (since Jaspers only had a doctorate *de rerum naturalium,* from the natural sciences), "We're proposing to award Jaspers an honorary doctorate, but we should ask him before doing it." (In the meantime Jaspers has indeed become an honorary doctor of philosophy.) Well, I had to go to Basel with my friend Schaefer, and I was treated shabbily there. Salin, a Georgian whom I knew well, was the rector there, and he was baffled. For when we got into a conversation, Jaspers said to Schaefer, "I would like to speak to you privately beforehand." Jaspers' wife was also there on this occasion, and she said, "But, Karl, you should speak with our old friend Gadamer, as well" — I was, after all, one of the ones who had been faithful to them. But he just answered, "Yes, yes, but he must wait a little." Then I was sent out, and I sat there for half an hour before I was summoned. You can imagine what a fascinating conversation we had! No, that was the end of it.

This was all a consequence of the baiting that I was subjected to into Heidelberg. But it was like this for everyone, so we don't need to waste any words over it. When one person leaves, then the group that remains considers the newcomer unacceptable — that's normal. The group is always naturally suspicious and unfriendly toward the new person, because they don't consider him to be of equal rank with the one who left.[2] This is simply a natural reaction to succession — which does stink to high heaven, but it's mainly out of jealously of the interloper. Of course, I always treated Roßmann and this Italian, de Rosa, who was also there, very politely — obviously. But, in spite of this, they always hated me, and so Jaspers always listened to the

---

2. Jean Grondin reports the same thing in his Gadamer biography (see *Hans-Georg Gadamer, Eine Biographie* (Tübingen, 1999), 304–13 [English translation: *Hans-Georg Gadamer: A Biography,* trans. Joel Weinsheimer (New Haven, Conn.: Yale University Press, 2003]). Meanwhile we know that the Jaspers' attitude toward Gadamer had, for other reasons and without Gadamer's knowledge, become critical, and no doubt because of Gadamer's rectoral address at the University of Leipzig in 1946. In this speech Jaspers saw signs of an accommodation by Gadamer to the communist regime of the GDR.

news about me by shaking his head and saying, "There's nothing new coming from old Gadamer." He was ambivalent on this point; it was just that he loved Roßmann, who later even became his successor — though certainly not through me.

D.: But Jaspers called you to Heidelberg anyway?

G.: No, he was barely in his office anymore. He didn't have any influence by that time. He did, of course, have a certain respect.

D.: Weren't you appointed to his position?

G.: No, I was only appointed afterwards — after he had already left. He wanted me, of course, but only as someone to visit him. It was an act of collegiality, so to speak — or whatever you want to call it. When I was a professor in Leipzig I naturally went to see him more often. But I only went to see Heidegger later — after he had come to his senses. As long as he was a Nazi, I never visited him. It simply would have been too awkward for me to do that by myself.

D.: Was Heidegger a Nazi to the end of the war?

G.: No, no. He hadn't been one for a long time before that. He had already stopped being a Nazi by the time he laid down his rectorship. There were probably certain residual traces that one could detect in him after that, but I had already known about it for a long time. He was always sending people to me in Marburg with this catchphrase: "This is a man you can really talk to." This kind of thing was quite usual at the time.

D.: Let's talk about the philosophical relationships between you and Jaspers now. What connected you to him?

G.: Well, in 1932 I received from Jaspers his little Göschen volume, *Über die geistige Situation unserer Zeit,* and I liked the introduction very much. It was an interesting introduction to the concept of the situation. On the whole, some things in it pleased me, others did not — and some of it smacked a little of Nazism, which was a sign of the times. Yet taken as a whole it was rather romantic and un-wittingly ironic — like when he says, "one raises one's spear and hits the mark," and such things. So I wasn't entirely enthusiastic, but it interested people. I did a seminar on it in Marburg. In that seminar I had almost the only Nazi-like reactions that I experienced during my entire tenure in Marburg from 1929 to 1935 — they were subtle, but quite unmistakable. So Jaspers did satisfy certain requirements of the Nazis, which was interesting for me to notice.

The other thing I didn't like about his character was that he was humorless. I experienced this personally when I was back here in Heidelberg. Once he was invited by the student body (not by the university) to give a talk, and I was asked to represent the rector. All of the other professors were angry with him. It was nothing special, nothing defamatory, just that he hadn't said goodbye when he went into retirement, and that was enough for the others to say, "If he wouldn't said goodbye to us, then we won't do anything for him either," and that's why I had to be there. So I came into the auditorium, which was very full, and my tongue slipped a couple of times as I said, "I come as a representative of the rector of the University of Leipzig. . . . " All I said was "Leipzig" instead of "Heidelberg." The others listened indulgently, and then there was some restlessness, and he said, "Leipzig? You're utterly mistaken!" Then I noticed it too and answered, "Leipzig? Oh, I'm terribly sorry! But you know, I was in this kind of situation so many times in Leipzig that something like this was bound to happen — and now it happens at exactly the wrong place. But, in any event, no one needs to come to you from Leipzig to tell you who Karl Jaspers is in Heidelberg." Then I blustered on. After that he became insecure for the first time. He had no humor at all, but I thought my turn of phrase was a rather elegant one — how nice it would have been had he been able to take it up. But he's not really like one would expect him to be. He could have said something . . . nothing! And, on top of that, it was a very bad lecture anyway.

Yet, in spite of all this, I did read his book *Das Gesetz des Tages und die Leidenschaft,* which was a reasonable reflection, and I later read his three volumes on philosophy with real admiration. Heidegger often sent me from Marburg to see him in Heidelberg, and, ultimately, when Jaspers was suddenly demoted, I traveled there from Leipzig all the more often. Persecuted people were all the same. In general they judged other people exclusively from one perspective — anyone who showed concern for them was something; anyone who proved himself useful was something special. Not entirely untrue — but I can't keep criticizing them like that. In any case, however, I was on the right side — on the side of those who showed concern. But it was also because I was aware of the great esteem that Heidegger had for

Jaspers. The break only happened later — because of Hitler. Incidentally, as you are probably already aware, a portion of Heidegger's rectoral address stems from Jaspers.

D.: Yes, I've read the Heidegger-Jaspers correspondence. There was a time (1930–32) during which they were very much in agreement.

G.: Not only that, but part of the material of the rectoral address comes from Jaspers. It's common knowledge that the ideas of labor service, military service, education service, and so on — all of that is Jaspers.

D.: Oh yes, the idea of the reform of the university — that was Jaspers' thinking.

G.: Yes, exactly.

D.: Nevertheless — if we could come back to the philosophical questions — what, in your opinion, are the differences and similarities between Heidegger and Jaspers? For example, with respect to the question of existence, do you think they had a uniform opinion on this, or did each one mean something different by it?

G.: They each meant something different by it — Heidegger meant "God."

D.: God?

G.: Yes, by existence, Heidegger meant the search for God. He was a seeker of God his entire life.

D.: But that's Kierkegaard's conception of existence!

G.: Quite right. At one point in his life he lost God, and so he spent his entire life searching for Him. But Jaspers — no, he didn't mean God; he meant "transcendence." They might be compatible to a certain extent. God knows, Jaspers wrote one of his best books about Kierkegaard and Nietzsche. The little book on Nietzsche was pretty good, but the big one wasn't — it was just pretty long.

D.: Kierkegaard defines existence as a standing out from one's own being and thus a being before God. Is this what Heidegger and Jaspers had in common?

G.: Yes, that was something common to them. But, in Heidegger's case, standing behind this idea was a man stamped by Catholicism who patiently sought God his entire life — right up to his death. He fell out with the church (even with his own faculty in Freiburg), fine; but he was quite human, all the same. He later encountered Protestantism and was inspired by it to come to Marburg, where he discovered the path of Bultmann and began a friendship with him (one with no ecclesiastical pressure), but this wasn't the right path either. And so on it went, and in the end it was Hölderlin. In fact, he was referred to as "Professor Hölderlin."

D.: Let's come back to the question of transcendence. Heidegger does speak about transcendence in his book *Kant and the Problem of Metaphysics,* and he equates it with the finitude of reason. That is to say, only from out of the finitude of the human being is there transcendence. Is this the same thing that Jaspers means or not?

G.: Well, that's what Jaspers says. Sure, sure, of course it's the same thing — but why? Being under the influence of the Enlightenment, Jaspers could speak of nothing but transcendence. Whereas Heidegger spoke of it because, at the moment, he didn't want to have anything to do with any church. This amounts to a distinction because one of them is seeing the tendency of the Enlightenment and the other is at odds with the established churches and their imperialism. For Heidegger there was no graver threat than the Confessing Church, which, on the contrary (in my opinion), really proved itself to be quite courageous in Nazi Germany.

D.: Courageous? How so?

G.: Yes, courageous. Hitler didn't penetrate into the villages and small towns — don't think they were nothing but Nazis.

D.: But didn't the church actually have its authority recognized by the Nazis?

G.: The pastors — the church didn't, but the pastors did — those village and small town pastors.

D.: Not the bishop of the Catholic Church as well?

G.: Bishops were unimportant to the Protestants.

D.: But we're still talking about Catholicism — about Heidegger's Catholicism.

G.: Oh, not any more. You misunderstood me. He had been on his quest for a long time when he got the call to Marburg, and this accounts for his friendship with Bultmann. But now I'm talking about the war, which broke out around this time and during which the church acted so bravely. Ultimately, neither Bultmann nor Protestantism satisfied him anymore. He didn't find any imperialism in it of the kind that he found in the Catholic Church, but he didn't find it very convincing either. Heidegger's thesis reads like this: "There is a God, to be sure, but there is no theology, nothing provable, nothing rational, or anything like it."

D.: In Jaspers' case, on the other hand, was there still a place for transcendence or for God?

G.: Yes, exactly. But he preferred to speak only of transcendence. As a matter of fact, he thought he had demonstrated this by means of the illumination of existence and by metaphysics, which one can derive (in a manner of speaking) from Kant. So Heidegger and Jaspers did have something in common — one of them as a victim of the Enlightenment and the other as a critic of ecclesiastical imperialism. He was already struggling against the authoritarianism of the Catholic Church as a child on the school bench. Do you know the story of him getting caught under the school bench?

D.: No, I don't know that one.

G.: Ah, it's a delightful story and it's even true. He was in high school in Konstanz and he was caught reading a book under the school bench during a boring lecture, and the one who caught him was Gröber, who later became bishop of Konstanz. The book was, of all things, Kant's *Critique of Pure Reason*. Gröber, being rather astute, was filled with respect. He praised Heidegger, and said to him, "I'd like to have more such students for whom I'm too boring and who prefer to read the *Critique of Pure Reason*!" He was a very honest and a very respectable man. But, of course, he was a also good Catholic. Later, when things became difficult, he helped Heidegger a lot — Heidegger went to Brentano on Gröber's recommendation. And, as a consequence of this episode, he began to occupy himself intensively with the various concepts of being (Brentano's famous book on Aristotle). That is really quite telling, isn't it? Simply out of interest, the young Heidegger read something more interesting than what Gröber was saying.

D.: Don't they say that when Gröber became bishop of Freiburg he had sympathies for the Nazis?

G.: When it comes to politics, one has to consider the Catholic Church in Germany as a whole — and there was the concordat. That was no private affair of Herr Gröber's. The politically influential bishops of the Catholic Church in Germany saw in it a chance to settle the Franciscan schism peacefully. We know, of course, that the Franciscans had fallen very much out of line. And, in point of fact, we also know about the repeated character assassination that was carried out by the Nazis. It came out in the newspapers during the second year of the Third Reich. I remember very precisely that it ended abruptly as criticism of the Franciscans broke off quite suddenly with the concluding of the concordat.

D.: But didn't all of this remain a secret?

G.: No, it was very public. This, of course, wasn't in the concordat itself; but evidently it did contain the freedom to worship and so on.

D.: But, after stepping down as rector, did Heidegger himself have difficulties with the Nazis?

G.: Of course he did. He saw things in a completely different way. Evidently he was very disappointed, and then — with the Arendt business — things got even worse for him. No, I would say that his bewilderment was now more in line with that of the Protestants, and, of course, he took Protestantism to be a watered-down form of religious faith. The political rhetoric of Catholicism was the opposite of this.

D.: This would have been a kind of imperialism, which Protestantism wasn't?

G.: Precisely, precisely. It was the opposite of imperialism, and he was quite rightly impressed by this. It was also a surprise to me. I was only able to see how superficial the whole influence of imperialism was when it came into contact with the petty bourgeoisie. This became clear to me during the years that I was living very quietly in Marburg — until all Hell broke loose. This is precisely why anti-Semitism makes me so exasperated these days. Now they're all talking about how to cope with the Holocaust. Some want this; others want that; some want a memorial; others want no memorial; still others think a small memorial would be right. This is all either dreadful or understandable, depending on how you look at it — but it's not about comprehending it. We really must understand once and for all how this happened against the will of an overwhelming majority of the Germans. Surely it was much the same in Italy. You didn't experience it firsthand, but, in all likelihood, the turn toward fascism in Italy was much the same.

D.: But let's come back to philosophy. We have now seen how you viewed the juxtaposition of Heidegger's and Jaspers' philosophies and their mutual relationship. Now we would like to talk about your own relationship to Jaspers. May I pose this question to you: What do you think you have learned from Jaspers?

G.: Well, as I see it, I learned something on the human level that, in Heidegger's case, was also present on the basis of his philosophy of existence. The fact that Heidegger was such a seeker of God became clear to me from the course of his life as a whole. For a while, at first, I even took him for someone who couldn't resist the Enlightenment any more and therefore no longer wanted to take part in all the tomfoolery of the game of Christianity. Yes, I have to admit that.

D.: What about this human side of existence? Do you understand by this the same thing that Habermas does when he says that hermeneutics is an urbanizing of Heidegger's thinking? Should this urbanizing be understood in the sense of human relationships, or should it be related above all to that quality of Heidegger's thinking that makes it so hard to communicate? Does Habermas just mean that you made it more communicable, that is, that you brought his thinking from his Black Forest hut into the city and made it understandable for people?

G.: No, I associated myself only with the human side of existence, just as Habermas does, I think. Incidentally, I'm reminded of a story that I often tell — it took place during a philosophy congress in Germany at which Ortega was present. Heidegger was apprehensive about getting into a discussion with Ortega. The open, extroverted, ironic manner in which Ortega spoke and discussed things always embarrassed him. He was quite aware of this himself and asked for my help the evening before. Actually, right after his lecture on the next day, Ortega made this ironic remark: "But, Herr Heidegger, you have to treat philosophy much more freely, more lightly — one must dance with philosophy." Heidegger said nothing. He withdrew into himself and murmured, "I really don't know what philosophy has to do with dancing."

D.: Now I would like to pose a philosophical question: Do you think that the illumination of existence has to do with hermeneutics, or is hermeneutics a different kind of philosophy altogether?

G.: Well, I'd say that the illumination of existence was a term for philosophy that even Heidegger accepted. He didn't exactly use it, but he didn't oppose it either.

D.: In Heidegger, in fact, don't we have the analytic of existence instead, which, in essence, is also to be distinguished from hermeneutics, just as the illumination of existence is in Jaspers' case?

G.: Yes. This is precisely why I say that, in Heidegger's case, truth is thought from within being, and I, in fact, don't do this. I almost consider that to be the erroneous fate of Western philosophy — the understanding of the human being that the Greeks established.

D.: Does this also apply to the illumination of existence?

G.: Yes, to that as well. That is, both the illumination of existence and the analytic of *Da-Sein* are attempts to think from out of the "Sein" instead of from out of the "Da." Heidegger later speaks of the "Da" as well, but by then I had long since arrived at it myself. I always thought it was wrong to say that he relied on Aristotle for this point. In my view, he disregarded *phronesis* and raised the question of being in its place.

D.: Hence the analytic of *Dasein* in Heidegger. Is this the same thing as the illumination of existence of which Jaspers speaks?

G.: Insofar as Jaspers even thought conceptually at all, one could answer this question very harshly. On the other hand, it is a very elegant expression — the illumination of existence — an expression that one understands immediately, but not one, in any case, that suggests a fundamental critique of the history of being in the West. But he took it to be a possibility that could triumph within the overall form of thinking. So, in the final analysis, he understood it in moralistic terms.

D.: You mean that the concept of the illumination of existence in Jaspers remains within the question of being and, to that extent, it also has to do with transcendence — even if it remains moralistic in the end?

G.: Yes, definitely. He had become somewhat more moralistic himself, but these days, all of a sudden, I find Jaspers wrongly being considered important. He wasn't really all that important.

D.: To what extent is he now considered important?

G.: One detects it everywhere. One notices it in every corner. Whenever we don't want to read Heidegger any more, we read Jaspers. This is clearly noticeable. But I'm also even-handed enough to say that there can be no doubt that both Heidegger and Jaspers were really exceptions in this drive to academicize philosophy in Germany. We have to acknowledge that about both of them.

D.: But didn't Jaspers, with his notion of the illumination of existence, touch at all upon the whole problem of the critique of metaphysics and Heidegger's new beginning in thinking, which in turn leads us to the authentic meaning of being, which is to say it leads us to transcendence?

G.: With respect to the contemporary situation, the illumination of existence, to me, is just a moralistic bourgeois term and not a religious meaning for transcendence. It is not transcendence in the sense of a church or a religion, but, instead, it remains within the influence of the Enlightenment, to which all of us are exposed as well. Plainly there are differences here — Heidegger was a religious person in this sense, while Jaspers was not.

D.: How, then, does hermeneutics distinguish itself from Heidegger's analytic of *Dasein,* on the one hand, and from Jaspers' illumination of existence, on the other?

G.: It seems to me that in Jaspers, in any case, there is rather too little meaning given to transcendence. On the other hand, however, it seems like a very difficult question to answer — it's as if you were asking me, "How should world history proceed?"

D.: No, I'm only asking where the difference really lay — irrespective of how history should proceed. How do you differ from Jaspers; how do you differ from Heidegger?

G.: No. You can't ask it like that either. Both questions are unimportant. What has become important is that this kind of upper-middle-class reserve of Jaspers couldn't save us. What could still save us, because we have nothing else, would be a conversation among the great religions.

D.: And not transcendence or philosophical faith in Jaspers' sense?

G.: No, that isn't nearly enough. We have to realize that the longing for transcendence that we have in our European thinking is secretly present everywhere and anywhere, and we must organize it in such a way that we can achieve comprehensively what, for instance, the Chinese have done with Shintoism. Is that too much to ask? How, then, could we do it? Well, perhaps we are already capable of it — if the four great world religions could reconcile themselves to acknowledging transcendence as "the great unknown," then they might even be able prevent the destruction of the earth's surface with gas and chemicals. Besides, it's the only way out — there is no other. We must enter into a conversation with the world religions. Maybe we have enough time; maybe we don't — I don't know. It might take a few centuries before it's possible to universalize a form of human rights in the Christian sense, so to speak, that is, in the sense in which we were brought up.

10
The Last God

D.: Now we'd like to talk about Heidegger again. Last time we talked about Jaspers; now we want to talk about Heidegger one more time. Do you think you correctly interpreted the concept of the thrownness of human beings in the world and that this constituted the beginning of your hermeneutic position?

G.: Yes, of course. And I'd say that I understood Heidegger as having seen something correct with the idea of thrownness. He saw that we must not look at everything from the perspective of logic. If I see that you are holding a glass in your hand, and I say, "Aha!" — then you, of course, have noticed that you are holding a glass, only you haven't formulated the *judgment* that you are holding the glass, while, generally speaking, I do consider myself as having formulated the judgment. This is why I wasn't at all astonished by the later Heidegger, whose thinking had to develop along these lines — it couldn't have worked out otherwise — when in the end he simply says, "It happens." But for a long time I have always put it like this: "I say *Sein* grudgingly, but I say *Da* quite willingly."

D.: Then doesn't this mean something like, "Being always limits itself to its historical presence"?

G.: Yes and no. Ultimately, being is really just a preliminary question.

D.: A preliminary question, and not a question about the truth of the proposition?

G.: That's the limit. That way of dealing with things is the limit in Heidegger. So, strictly speaking, I don't believe that the truth of being that he talks about can be confused with the truth of the proposition — especially if one means its verifiability by means of propositional truth. It's clear that the originary evidence of being, *aletheia,* is something different. Up to now, I still haven't found any answer to this. But you know what Heidegger said to his family over and over again during the last years of his life — "Nietzsche has broken me."[1]

D.: What did he mean by that?

G.: I don't know. You can't tease it out of Hermann Heidegger. He wasn't well enough trained in philosophy to explain why his father repeated the statement over and over, "Nietzsche has broken me." I can't explain it rationally either. I don't have an answer — or perhaps I should say, I have few answers; I ponder the question quite often. Arthur Danto, in the meantime, has published a book on Nietzsche — he sent me a copy and wrote a very, very nice dedication in it. In my opinion, at least, he's a man to be taken seriously, and perhaps he suspected an answer.

D.: What do you think Heidegger meant by this dictum about Nietzsche? Do you really have no explanation for it?

G.: No, I still don't have any firm conviction about it. I think that to see certain things when we read Heidegger's Nietzsche volumes (which, of course, Otto Pöggler edited), one must always remember that this is already a pre-digested Heidegger. Now we finally have the complete edition of the lectures. The lectures as Heidegger originally delivered them are much better than the two volumes that Pöggler edited.

D.: Really? Are you sure that the two volumes are worse than the lectures?

G.: Yes, they aren't nearly as important. Stylistically speaking, Heidegger was really not a very good writer — and I say that with absolute conviction. And I'm not alone in saying things like this. These days, actually, anyone who can read these lectures says the same thing. At the moment, however, I don't know whether the same thing can be said of Hegel. We don't yet have a really good edition of Hegel, while we do have one now of Heidegger; and that's why I would say it's a good thing.

D.: Then, does Heidegger's actual lecture come to the fore in this edition?

G.: Most definitely.

---

1. [*Nietzsche hat mich kaputtgemacht.*]

D.: Just the way you heard it in Marburg?

G.: Yes, yes. It's infinitely better. By the way, I must say that, generally . . . no, no — of course, I have always thought that Heidegger definitely had an enormous philosophical imagination. I understood this as soon as I saw his eyes for the first time. I told you how I had to introduce myself to him when I went to Freiburg, and I peeked into the university and saw that a door was opening in the distance. Presently, a small man came out leading a larger man. Then he shut the door again. It never occurred to me that it could be him. I waited for a long time. Finally, I knocked; then the smaller man came to the entrance, and it was Heidegger. I was very impressed by his gaze.

D.: Was it a deep gaze?

G.: An imaginative gaze. I stayed only a few minutes, and he asked if I wanted to write an essay with him. In those days he actually considered me to be enormously talented, which was very candid of him. He had always hoped to find someone from among his students to help him. Then, at the end of my studies, when I was twenty-three years old, he tried very hard to get me to work with him or at least to become his assistant. Later, when he realized what he had been suggesting, he soon dropped me again. That wasn't a bad thing. It didn't matter to me, and as a result I told myself that I now had to learn to do something that he couldn't do — and so I became a classical philologist. This rankled Heidegger. He hadn't advised me to do this; I advised myself to do it. So I could now do something that he couldn't do. And, let there be no doubt about it, whenever he came to me now with interpretations of Greek texts, I took every opportunity to drive home the fact that he didn't have enough Greek. That's just how things were — although, obviously I will always appreciate the fact that I would never have experienced the Greeks so vividly without Heidegger. When, for example, he reads the Presocratics . . . well, in this case, if he really wants to hide behind the Presocratics, then fine — I can even see a motive for it. But ultimately he has to make the attempt not to mistreat the language of the Anaximander fragment in that way — it's absolutely barbarous.

D.: So, you don't agree with his interpretation of Anaximander at all?

G.: I wouldn't say that. I would just say that, in this case — with this fragment — you should really sit down and deal with the corresponding interpretation from Aristotelian philosophy before you can begin talking about it at all. He doesn't really do that. You know my little Reklam volume about the beginning of Western philosophy — it becomes a little more concrete there, I think, because I actually discovered a Heraclitus fragment. It's the last one in the list of Hippolytus, the Cynic. Heraclitus' statements were very much in circulation at the time, and Hippolytus collected them. But his last one was always left out because it was considered bogus since it echoes the Trinity too much. The statement reads, "The father himself only becomes a father in that he produces a son."[2] [In the original,] Hippolytus expresses himself in terms of the Trinity. This is why the philologists removed it. I have only recently discovered this — it isn't in the Heraclitus chapter of *The Fragments of the Presocratics*. But even though I'm the one who pulled this out of the text, I submit to you that it is still perfectly Heraclitean — "The father only *becomes* a father, in that he has a son." It becomes clear the moment you hear it. How odd that no one else has hit upon this. We have now one more magnificent statement from Heraclitus.

D.: Heraclitus' statements used to be understood only in terms of opposition. This one has the ring of a Hegelian mediation.

G.: Yes, but that hasn't always been the case either, for there are still many other forms. In fact, this isn't actually Heraclitus himself, but rather a description. Nevertheless, it describes exactly what you correctly say is not found in the other statements from Heraclitus but, instead, only ever occurs in terms of oppositions in parts of the sentences. All in all, I believe my Heraclitus essay is quite correct. But it isn't anything entirely new; I just had it reprinted for this popular

2. Cf. Hans-Georg Gadamer, "Von Anfang bei Heraklit," *Gesammelte Werke* 6 (Tübingen: J. C. B. Mohr, 1985), 232–41). Reprinted as "Von der Überlieferung Heraklits" in *Der Anfang des Wissens* (Reklam, 1999) [this is the "popular edition" to which Gadamer refers below. The essay has been translated into English as "On the Tradition of Heraclitus" in *The Beginning of Knowledge,* trans. Rod Coltman (New York: Continuum 2002), 21–32. In Gadamer's German translation,] the complete statement from Hippolytus reads, "Solange der Vater nicht ins Werden eingegangen war, kann er mit Recht Vater genannt werden. Als er aber sich herabließ, Werden auf sich zu nehmen, gezeugt wurde der Sohn, er selbst von sich selber und nicht von jemand anderem" [or, in English, "So long as the father did not come into being, can he rightly be named father. However, when he condescended to take becoming upon himself, he became the son of himself and not of someone else."] According to Gadamer's interpretation, the expression, "when he condescended to take becoming upon himself," could [never] be genuinely Heraclitean. [Note: The original German of the present volume omits Gadamer's "never." This sentence fragment is actually part of what Gadamer calls the original statement's "Christian veneer," which needs to be stripped away to reveal the Heraclitean idea that Gadamer cites here.]

edition, which is an experience that I never get excited about — that is, when you print something in a volume of collected writings that until then hadn't been published anywhere else, and it comes out yet again in a popular edition.

D.: As you told us earlier, after your first crisis with Heidegger, your relationship with him then went back to the way it was before?

G.: Yes, after having done my examinations with him he wanted me to do my habilitation thesis with him as well since he suspected that, otherwise, Friedländer would gladly have done it with me. To my greatest joy I recently heard — just a few days ago, now — that, in one of Heidegger's last letters to Hannah Arendt, he says, "You must read Gadamer's *Wahrheit und Methode* and Volume III of his *Kleine Schriften*." This is the volume that contains my essay, "The Phenomenological Movement — Husserl and Heidegger." This last reference didn't amaze me so much, but the first one really did — it's the only time that Heidegger ever expresses himself positively about *Truth and Method*.

D.: So, you don't really have any explanation for what Heidegger could have meant by his pronouncement about Nietzsche having broken him?

G.: I haven't a clue. I only heard about it for the first time when Hermann Heidegger told me that he kept repeating over and over again to the end of his days, "Nietzsche has broken me." Had he fallen apart, had he become shipwrecked upon Nietzsche's thinking — who can say? Perhaps he had realized that he couldn't make Nietzsche into the last metaphysician after all, and that would probably have cast doubt on his whole conception or construction of Western philosophy as a history of metaphysics that he would subsequently dismantle.

D.: Then this history of metaphysics, understood as the history of being or even as the ontological destiny of the West [*Seins-Geschick des Abendlandes*], would have been brought to a head by Nietzsche's absolute will to power. But then it would collapse in on itself when Nietzsche's absolute will to power — which constitutes the inverse of absolute knowing in Hegel — could no longer be understood as an absolute metaphysical principle. Just as history — in the form of absolute knowing — is included in Hegel, so history should also be included in Nietzsche's absolute principle of the will to power. This would indeed be the case if one were to interpret history as the process of the eternal recurrence of the same. And the reason why Heidegger had to understand the eternal recurrence as the other side of the will to power was because of the inner coherence of his interpretations of Hegel and Nietzsche. Do you actually think that Heidegger might have become shipwrecked upon Nietzsche because he realized the impossibility of this interpretation? Do you yourself believe that this interpretation — which so closely links the will to power and the eternal recurrence of the same — is actually untenable?

G.: Yes, I do, in fact, believe that this interpretation is no longer tenable. The eternal recurrence of the same doesn't have this significance in Nietzsche at all — just as the will to power cannot be understood as a metaphysical principle. Contrary to all of the cosmological interpretations, I have long proposed my own interpretation of the eternal recurrence of the same — it stems from the state of deep despair that Nietzsche was in during the time that he was writing *Thus Spoke Zarathustra*. He had even planned his suicide at the end of the third book. One of the plans for the final draft of the book actually contained the death of Zarathustra. This is also what is told to us indirectly at the end of the third book when in the last part of "The Other Dancing Song" Zarathustra's dialogue with life is described as a conversation of the soul with itself. Life, that is, says to Zarathustra, "You do not love me nearly so much as you say. I know you are thinking that you will leave me soon." "But no one knows that," answers Zarathustra.[3] Finally, overwhelmed by the sadness of the sunset, Zarathustra and Life weep together. But the definitive conclusion of the third book, in the section entitled "The Seven Seals," will bid us, "Sing, speak no more!" The will to life, the love of life, confronts the wisdom of self-consciousness, which is aware of its own death. Knowledge of the necessity of transience and death confronts itself in the eternal recurrence of the same just as much as the will to eternity does. One cannot solve this conflict through the wisdom of self-consciousness — through *logos,* or through words — but only by singing, whereby one attains the innocence of the child at play again. This exhortation to sing is the one possible victory over death, the overcoming of which lies in the acceptance of the eternal recurrence — as sad and difficult as this overcoming can be. It is this desire

---

3. [These words, "Das weiß niemand," are actually spoken to Zarathustra by Life after he whispers something into her ear.]

for the eternity of life and not a metaphysical theory that is affirmed by the pronouncement, "Sing, speak no more!"[4]

D.: But if, in the end, Heidegger had also recognized all of this and, consequently, the impossibility of making Nietzsche into the last metaphysician or the consummation of Western metaphysics, then I don't think this would have caused him go to pieces over Nietzsche. If we want to seek another explanation, then perhaps we could take into consideration what you said about Heidegger being a man who was always searching for God. Don't you think that Nietzsche might have broken him in this respect, since Nietzsche speaks precisely of the definitive death of God?

G.: It's possible, of course, that this idea of the death of God represented a trauma — not only for his thinking but, in fact, also for his life. But one can get nothing out of his son, Hermann Heidegger. I saw Heidegger himself just a few days before his death. I was in Freiburg, and I visited him at home. He came downstairs with his wife to greet me, and later we drank a marvelous wine (he was always receiving very good wines as gifts from his devoted admirers, and was no longer allowed to drink as much). But, philosophically speaking, he definitely did not think too highly of me.

D.: What did he say to you when you saw him for the last time?

G.: Well, he began like this: "You say that language is a conversation, no?" "Yes," I answered. It began like this, but it didn't go much further because I just don't have the gift that you displayed that time in Heidelberg.[5] You knew exactly what he was driving at and always had a reply for it. It wasn't like that in my case. If I had managed to get myself involved in the question, then perhaps we would have gone further, and it might have resulted in an interesting conversation in connection with his essay "On the Way to Language." You, on the other hand, corroborated him, so to speak, step-by-step. Yes, that made him quite happy. Well, now I have learned to appreciate how you did that — only I can't change the way I am. I just didn't have the talent for it. In fact, you can see this in all my writings — most

4. Relevant to this entire section, see Hans-Georg Gadamer, "Nietzsche-der Antipode. Das Drama Zarathustras" (1984) now in *Gesammelte Werke*, vol. 4 (Tübingen 1987), 458–62.

5. This refers to the seminar that was held in 1970 in Heidelberg on the day of Gadamer's seventieth birthday, which Heidegger attended and where I answered all of the questions posed by Heidegger in such a way that a lively discussion ensued.

people can just say something; then they can talk about it and make it vivid, but there's no such pre-structured program in me.

D.: But in this last conversation didn't you get around to speaking with him about Nietzsche and his being shipwrecked with him?

G.: Oh, no. I didn't know about that yet. I only heard about it after his death.

D.: But, getting back to his ideas about a new god, perhaps we should think that this new god — or the last god — is supposed to come after the death of God, which was announced by the madman in Nietzsche's *Gay Science* and which Heidegger simply interpreted as a death of the Christian God. We might also think that the new god represents precisely a new direction in humanity's own path — the path that humanity must take after its loss of faith in the Christian God. Would the last god, then, be the authentic thought of the divine that is present in all religions — that is to say, transcendence without Christian theology or without any form of theology, which died along with the Christian God?

G.: Perhaps. But I'm not entirely certain. I can't give you a definitive answer.

D.: But if people are turning away from Heidegger now and want to read Jaspers again, why is that? Doesn't the reason lie precisely in the distinction between Heidegger's analysis of *Dasein* and Jaspers' illumination of existence and whatever constitutes this distinction?

G.: The difference is in the radical way in which Heidegger clarified the false move that Western thinking has made from being to the world, from being to beings. In essence, Jaspers has circumvented this — albeit in a lyrical way — by invoking the idea of the illumination of existence to express himself on the matter, and he didn't see how much Heidegger's analytic of *Dasein* and his insistence upon *Dasein* constitute a critique of being as it had been understood by Western metaphysics. I think you still have to see this much more sharply — in the end, from Jaspers' point of view, we might even take Heidegger for an imaginative madman. Do we really want to revoke this false move and assume that it was all wrong so we can perhaps go back to Parmenides? Heidegger thinks through this whole process of the history of Western thought by proceeding backward from its end. Even I thought this might work with Parmenides until Rickert showed me that it wouldn't.

D.: Are you referring to Rickert's famous book on the various meanings of the one, in which the mathematical one is differentiated from the one as a metaphysical principle, just as the whole of what is is differentiated from oneness?[6] Didn't Heidegger (and you yourself, so far as I know) esteem Rickert far more for this work than on the basis of his philosophy of values?

G.: Yes, certainly.

D.: I remember quite clearly how Heidegger himself, who had traveled to Heidelberg for your birthday, participated in one of your last seminars in the Winter of 1970. In the middle of the seminar, directly in relation to the transcendental unity of apperception, he posed the question, "What is meant here by the concept of the one?" My answer was that being must be considered as something uniform and must be traced back to a unitary center if it is to be thought at all. He shook his head and said simply, "But, why, in originary Greek thinking, does being become the one? I freely admit that I haven't gotten to the bottom of that one."[7] So, do you also think that being and the one are not the same thing and that Parmenides' *eon* doesn't mean that the *on*, what is, and the *hen*, the one, are unified within themselves? This is why one can't see the beginning of Western metaphysics or Western science in Parmenides.

G.: I have to go farther back to find the beginning of Western science — it's already there with the Sumerians. Although it's true that there is still no mathematics (and I have said this before) until Greek science comes along — only then does one get mathematical formulas. In the case of the Egyptians, what they had in this regard wasn't strictly science, but rather an expertise in measurement. If Heidegger had been more open or more consistent, then he could have seen this difficulty, and he might have differentiated philosophical or metaphysical thinking from an exact science as well as from a science that makes the whole of what is into an object of recognition and measurement.

6. See Heinrich Rickert, *Das Eine, die Einheit und die Eins*, 2d ed. (Tübingen: J. C. B. Mohr [Paul Siebeck], 1924).

7. I have published a record of this session. See Riccardo Dottori, "Kritisches Nachwort zu "Hegels Dialektik" von Hans-Georg Gadamer und zum Verhältnis Hegel-Heidegger-Gadamer," in *Bijdragen*, 38 (1977): 176–92.

Now Heidegger was always dismissive in his behavior toward me — he always said, "Well, of course, he always does everything with hermeneutics." And yet, of course, things are a little different than he imagined them to be. It's just not true that I think I'm making up a new philosophy. I'm speaking to you kids when I say this. Admit it — you no longer know anything. But I think Socrates would say this too. In fact, I need to say something in reference to your compatriots now as well — Viano and the others — why don't you see this? I just don't understand it. There wasn't really a system at all — these Tübingen people are just crazy. I can't detect any systems in philosophy prior to the seventeenth century. This is a formulation that first occurs in Suárez.

D.: Not entirely in Suárez, I believe. He did formulate a system, but he didn't talk about systems. I think the first one to use the term was the Cartesian who first introduced the term "ontology," which subsequently became the basis for a system.

G.: That's almost correct, though not quite. But one can see that the idea begins here in principle. Besides (and once again I have checked this out thoroughly), there isn't a single example in philosophy in which the word *systhema* presents itself. It has to do with the stars, it has to do with musical tones, and all sorts of things — but it really has nothing to do with philosophy.

D.: Well, these days it seems like philosophy once again wants nothing to do with systems. But, on the other hand — provided we're trying to do plain analytical philosophy — philosophy is no longer about searching for certainties. Instead, its about ultimate answers to the meaning of life, the world, and the human being. Do you think that the question of the meaning of being, which in Heidegger becomes the question of the last god, ultimately moves in this direction?

G.: Yes, I think Heidegger thought that the Industrial Revolution would prove itself so intolerable that it would result in a new solidarity among human beings and perhaps a new god as well.

D.: This would be the last god?

G.: Yes, I had a conversation with him about this.

D.: The last god or the new god?

G.: No, the new god. That is, I asked him once, "Why did you leave your posthumous papers to that national archive in Marbach? After all, one can't work properly with your things there at all — they don't have a philosophical library." "Yes, yes," he said, "I know that, of course. I could have left it all to the Freiburg library where I was a professor. But ultimately I found out from my son that they have very deep treasure troves in Marbach where many treasures are buried." "Did there have to be?" I asked. "No," he replied, "but my writings aren't all that important now." "Apparently not," I said. "No," he answered, "what's important to me is that we now arrive at a new direction — that humanity achieve a new kind of solidarity."

D.: And would that be unthinkable from Jaspers' perspective?

G.: Oh yes.

D.: So you think that hermeneutics should be grasped as an understanding between religions and cultures, and you think that Heidegger promises us more along these lines than Nietzsche does?

G.: I am convinced that this is how the conversation will have to be carried out. It's the only way out — there's no other way.

D.: Then not even a faith in the Enlightenment (in Jaspers' sense) or even a psychologizing of faith?

G.: No, no, that's not it. I'm really talking about a religious dialogue about transcendence, if you will. I wouldn't claim that the same things that I see can't be described with Jaspers' concept of transcendence. But it is mainly a function of the Enlightenment being *our* concern and not a concern of the entire world. And it would still bring us much that is remarkable if, let's say, we were to bring ourselves to an understanding with Islam, which, at the moment, is the most difficult thing of all but also, in a certain sense, the most essential. There's a huge difference between us right now, but, ultimately, there's a right and a left in the Islamic world, too. There's even a movement there that doesn't just stick strictly to what it had previously learned — it says, "We need to adapt ourselves to the modern world — we could risk it." I could imagine this, but, of course, I have no right to believe it because we are still too far away from such a thing. Nevertheless, I would like to defend one single assertion — the idea that angst is a natural instinct that everyone possesses. Since we are in the highly unfortunate situation of having our survival depend on our behavior, we are deeply plagued by angst. So says the famous passage from Schelling that Heidegger so often quoted, "The angst of life drives creatures away from their center."

D.: Is this the same angst that is described in Heidegger's analysis of existence, or are you referring to a completely different one?

G.: I don't know if it's the same one. What has become clear to me, however, is that Heidegger was a deeply religious man and a frustrated thinker — in this respect, of course — and that he knew this about himself. But that doesn't mean that what he thought is wrong — he was on the right path in the analysis of human existence. He had a great deal of imagination, whereas Jaspers was not so imaginative — there was a certain foolishness in his thinking.

D.: So would you say that the illumination of existence is a psychologizing analysis of the human being?

G.: Yes, and of bourgeois morality. Jaspers was much more bourgeois than he thought. Heidegger, on the other hand, was just a peasant.

D.: Is that why he had a more direct connection with nature, whereas Jaspers was a man of the city, and that's why the urbanizing of hermeneutics was more likely to occur in Jaspers?

G.: Yes, absolutely. But, I'm a little surprised that you are playing Jaspers up so much — it doesn't make sense to me. Actually, for a long time I asked myself (entirely within the framework of your question) whether the illumination of existence wouldn't be a nice, elegant formulation for Heidegger — no doubt it would. Meanwhile, I look at how different things have become today. In essence, we are headed directly toward a global crises. And, after having seen to it that we ourselves — by way of science — have threatened to destroy life on this planet, we must ask ourselves whether there's anything to prevent us from allowing something like that to occur. It's not very likely. We tried not to overestimate atomic energy, but meanwhile the advancements in chemistry are so enormous that I can very well imagine that the planet's destruction won't begin with a first strike.[8] So I think it's inevitable that a Saddam Hussein or somebody will try it — humanity will expect nothing less. If it happens just once,

---

8. [Gadamer presumably means that a nuclear attack is not as likely at the moment as an attack from chemical weapons of mass destruction.]

if the earth suffers such a disaster just once, be it from atomic energy or from chemical materials, then perhaps weapons can succeed in getting us to work out the fine points of our problem after all — ideologies succeed at nothing.

D.: So, enlightenment alone will not suffice? According to Jaspers it would.

G.: No, it isn't enough. That is, I think humanity is more likely to go down this semi-catastrophic road. It might even become an epidemic that one cannot control, that one cannot predict. Anything at all could make it so that our angst brings humanity to a halt. If angst, as it were, threatens everyone, then perhaps there is hope that people will come to an understanding of some sensible conception of transcendence — perhaps people will begin asking themselves why we are born without being asked, why we die without being asked, and so on.

D.: Those are religious questions, aren't they?

G.: Yes, in the final analysis, they are religious questions.

D.: And, until now, has religion perhaps made the mistake of wanting to impose its standards on humanity, of wanting to dominate it, or (in Heidegger's terms) of being "imperialistic"?

G.: Yes, this abuse occurs again and again throughout the whole of theology.

D.: Do we want to end our conversations with this indictment of theology?

G.: No, I have nothing against theology, which, especially in Germany, played a large role within the political and cultural debate at the time of the Reformation and contributed very much to the honing and the refinement of sensibilities about religious, ethical, and philosophical problems, not to mention the origin of hermeneutics. I only want to warn of the misuse that one makes of a theological doctrine when it turns into an instrument of the imperialism of a church within a state. The blame rests not with theology as such, but with the subjection of theology to a doctrine and of the concomitant religious sentiment being subjected to the power of a church.

D.: What, in your opinion, is religious sentiment otherwise?

G.: An unavoidable question for us — a hope perhaps, or, rather, a task that unites us all in our mutual understanding. This ultimate ethical task cannot be separated from the one task of questioning and understanding our own existence.

Portrait and Dialogue

The Gadamer portrait by Dora Mittenzwei, entitled ὁ φιλόσοφος αὐτος, was unveiled in Heidelberg on March 21, 2002. In the presence of numerous representatives of the university and of the city of Heidelberg, Professor Riccardo Dottori gave the address that follows below. The publishing house is grateful for permission to reproduce both the portrait and the text.

A picture, if it is a work of art, is neither the glorification of an individual person nor an objective representation — if there is such a thing — of the image of a person or a personality. What then is the purpose of a work of art, and what, in particular, is the intention of a portrait that claims to be a work of art?

Does a work of art originate, perhaps, from a desire for liberation from the limitations of everyday reality — from the desire to transcend the actual — or, to put it in Kantian terms, from a lack of interest in what is useful, from the will to intensify the desire for life and the will to life (as in Nietzsche)? We can see how, in modern art, the work of art disrupts the superficial external appearance of things or of the world in order to go into more depth or to intensify the potential for contemplation and perception and to create and communicate something new via the image. The shock effect or the challenge that results from this disruption of the usual appearance serves to refine our senses and to magnify our capacities. One might see the truth value of a work of art by speaking (as Heidegger does) of an encounter with true being.

Does all of this also apply to a portrait? Or do we have to look at a portrait from a different angle, that is, from our desire to preserve the familiar image of a person close to us even when that person is no longer available to our senses and has been taken from us, either by the various circumstances of life or through death? Do we need the portrait to keep that person's appearance and presence not only in our memory but also in front of our eyes so that we can still experience a kind of familiar togetherness with it, so that we can, as they say, "live with the picture"? But is the same thing not also achieved or brought about by every picture or every photograph?

Here we see how an image as a work of art differs from the objective rendering created by modern technical reproduction. Today, we ascribe a certain artistic value to photography in that we assume — or photography itself assumes — that it is not a sheer technical reproduction but rather the being of that which it represents, and that, in a certain way, it enriches what it represents and allows it to come forth in ever new aspects and shadings. This is surely the case, and, in fact, it was something that was first brought out by Gadamer himself. The photograph, however, cannot go beyond new shadings of the being of what is depicted in order to continue playing with the light cast on the subject, the face, or an aspect of the subject — instead it depends entirely, if you will, on the object or the subject, because the look of the photograph has to present itself and is not brought out by the action of an artist.

The painter's portrait, however, is different. The painter creates the look, the appearance, the expression, the attitude, the manner, and the bearing of the person represented or portrayed from out of him- or herself. All of this is the product of free creation, if one can even call it a "product" as in a photographic reproduction. But we do not say "product" or "reproduction." We refer instead to the "work" of an artist, and we mean by this that everything in it depends on the artist and is brought forth by the artist. The person depicted is his or her work of art. One might object by asking, "What is this work, exactly? What is created through this work?"

Did we not speak earlier, in Heideggerian terms, about the true being that is presented through art? But how can this true being be preserved if the artist puts his or her own work in its place? Should we not say, instead, that the artist alters the true being of the one portrayed and replaces it with his or her own intention and his or her own image?

The tradition of portraiture teaches us that every portrait, every head, every bust or statue has always been an interpretation and has always depended on the fashion of the time, the reigning ideology, or the personal predilections of the artist. In antiquity, the portrait or statue is always a glorification of the king or ruler, of the great general who stands there in his masterful pose with his gaze peering into the far reaches of the field to be defended or conquered, or simply toward the distant future and the fate of his land. We recall how all of this changes in the Christian era when it is replaced by the suffering gaze of Jesus or Mary or some saint — a figure that, in its suffering gaze and in its gesture of resigned acceptance, nevertheless promises redemption. Finally, we recall how, in the Renaissance, in place of the suffering figure we find the human being who stands there in a world presented in perspective and how, even in his entirely individual gaze, he is nevertheless depicted as the center of the universe. It is actually the discovery of subjectivity and self-awareness that reflects itself in the central perspective, and this discovery brings us closer to the psychologizing analysis of the subject that we find in a Rembrandt, a Velázquez, or a Goya, until later (in the Rococo period) this subjectivity, having been absorbed into the human soul, fades away again and finally passes over into the genre portrait.

What kind of lesson should we draw from this development of portraiture in the history of our culture? What does it have to do with the above-mentioned dictum of Heidegger and Gadamer that art should understand and express the truth of being? Should we not say, instead, that art is an interpretation that is constantly changing itself, an interpretation that subjects itself to the flow of time? Ever since Gadamer, we have known that a constantly changing interpretation does not impair the demands of truth; rather, it allows ever newer aspects of self-showing being to come forth. And yet, I do not think we come close to the importance of the portrait even with this. We only learn its true significance from the later history of portraiture.

The renewed task of the spirit of modern art was to dissolve the immediacy of the genre portrait and to replace the familiar image with something entirely different; we can no longer recognize the person portrayed in a picture — or, at least, not at first glance. We are aware of the famous distinction that is made here between the acknowledging and the recognizing gaze. The image becomes totally disguised or distorted, or there might even be an entirely different sign of recognition that is displayed as the portrait in place of the image. I assume that many people are familiar with the famous exhibition of Picasso and his women that was organized at the Museum of Modern Art in New York by the director emeritus and famous art historian William Rubin. The subtitle of the exhibition was "Representation and Interpretation."[1] The title thus affirms Rubin's opinion

1. [The full title of the exhibition was actually "Picasso and Portraiture: Representation and *Transformation*" rather than "Representation and *Interpretation*." William Rubin also wrote a book entitled *Picasso and Portraiture* (Thames and Hudson, 1996), to accompany the show.]

that these deformed representations of the women whom Picasso loved were an interpretation. However, by "interpretation" [*die Interpretation*] — be it the interpretation of texts or works, or expressions of the words of others or of the word of God — we typically mean personal interpretation [*die persönliche Auslegung*] or representation in our language and through our understanding. Interpretation is always either a translation from one language into another or a representation of something we have seen, or heard, or read. This representation, of course, presupposes our understanding and is achieved by our understanding — therein lies the possibility of a deepening of that understanding and a personal penetration into the interpreted phenomenon, be it a book, a law, a piece of music, an object of our knowledge, an event, a complex association of events, or the entire world. All of this understanding presupposes critique and is either expressed in the interpreting or is itself the critical interpretation. This also may hold true for works of art, which are themselves a personal, that is to say, a critical interpretation of what is represented before they themselves are subjected to the critical interpretation of the art critic. With a portrait, however, we are dealing with something different, and the best way to learn about this difference is through a portrait like this one, which has an excellent subject — a philosopher or *ho philosophos autos*.

In dozens of his portraits, Picasso studies the face, the figure, the expression, and the look of his Marie Therese and deforms them arbitrarily — that is, not in an arbitrary manner, but in such a way as to arbitrarily allow something essential of her character, her spirit, the sense of her personality, and her unique nature to emerge in each instance by means of this deformation. This presupposes not only one view or one aspect of the person portrayed, but rather a deep commonality with her, a genuine communicating, or, as we might say, a dialogue — even if it be that silent dialogue with a loved one that happens through looks and that we all know so well, a dialogue that perhaps says more than any spoken word and that may even be represented better through an image (if we are capable of it), that is, through the portrait. Just as in the process of interpretation of which we were speaking earlier, there is more to becoming engrossed in the gaze of another than there is in being engrossed in just any phenomenon.

The object of our interpretation may well be a text, a complicated state of affairs, or a phenomenon into which we are meant to transpose or engross ourselves, but in each case it is always question of a guessing or a comprehending of this or that — our object always remains what is interpreted, even if it is an event. This is not the case, however, in a dialogue where the living person stands before us and where we are not only listening to their words and trying to guess their meaning but where, by means of their gaze, we can actually look into and penetrate the soul of the other. Our answer or our question is the fruit of this penetration into the dialogue — this well-intentioned linguistic access to the other that one communicates and performs in the conversation. For an artist, this access can be even more intense — in this case, the answer or fruit of the penetration is the portrait.

Thus the portrait is itself a conversation, the representation of the well-intentioned entry into the soul of the other and of the secret that one has brought to light through the gaze of the other and its reciprocation. Every portrait presupposes this gradual access to the other, this quiet conversation of the eyes and the gaze, and not merely the psychological observation and analysis that has arisen through some important portraits that belong to the bygone history of portraiture and its historically conditioned pre-understanding. What we have before of us in this portrait of the philosopher himself, of course, is an even more propitious case, and for two reasons: First, Gadamer himself was the philosopher who proposed dialogue as the meaning of both his philosophy and his personal view of life. Second, we can say (along with Plato) that philosophy itself, the search for truth, is a dialogue and becomes manifest in the dialogue. The *philosophos autos,* therefore, had to be depicted in the attitude of dialogue and living conversation, and we see here that the artist did indeed touch upon and depict the soul of Gadamer, the sense of his personality and his philosophy — from a quiet conversation with him, the essence of both the philosopher himself and his philosophy became manifest to her as a dialogue.

So, in this example, art shows us not how (through its own unique work) it puts something else in place of what is true, but rather how it allows the truth of its essence or its being to shine forth — neither as objectively rendered reproduction nor as a merely subjective interpretation. Any interpretation is a true interpretation if it uncovers the essential and makes it manifest in the being of what it interprets without merely explicating the object. This is also the case in art. It always shows us something essential, and yet it always shows us something new.

But we can also see how it works differently in portraiture as compared to other genres of the art (painting, that is); in its work, it does not just allows its object, that is, the soul of the one portrayed, to emerge in such a way that it puts something else — something of its own — in its place. Because the portrait is a dialogue and has to do with an exchange with the living spirit of the other, it is primarily concerned with allowing the authentic spirit of the other, his or her radiant truth to emerge or, as Heidegger would say, to bring it into the unconcealed.

So much for the artist and what he or she depicts — but, what about us, the viewers? What effect does the work intend to have on us, what effect *should* it have on us with its representation addressing us with such brilliant colors? What is the beautiful — that which pleases us? Is it perhaps participation in this silent conversation that speaks only by glances or looks? Is this "pleasing" merely the expression, the sensory sign or evidence of our participating in something in such a way that we are thereby enjoying ourselves, as Kant certainly thought? Perhaps. But perhaps it is something more. In this particular case, where we all know the one portrayed and where we are so connected to him, we still have the impression of being able to continue participating in this conversation — even though the living presence is lost. This image is so successful that we will always have the depicted spirit before us, and we will continue to participate in this conversation as long as we are allowed to stand in front of the image and observe it.

This is why we are grateful to the artist who evoked this conversation in the image and put it into work. We are grateful to the donor who, through her donation, makes it possible for us to continue living with the image. We are grateful for the joy that it affords us and for the anticipation of being able to have Gadamer constantly before us in his dialogical attitude and to continue participating with him in his dialogue.

Index